GREAT BATTLES OF WORLD WAR I:

In the Air

GREAT BATTLES OF WORLD WAR I:

In the Air

◎ ◎ ◎ ◎ ◎ ◎ ◎ ◎ ◎

Compiled by FRANK C. PLATT

Weathervane Books • New York

CONTENTS

GREAT BATTLES OF WORLD WAR I:

In the Air

Bishop of the Eagle Eye

BY A. ROY BROWN

(Editor's Note: Captain Brown, a native Canadian like Bishop, was himself a famous air fighter—officially credited with the killing of Baron von Richthofen, the greatest German ace, on April 21, 1918.)

◎ ◎ ◎ ◎ ◎ ◎ ◎ ◎ ◎

THE greatest living, fighting airman is Billy Bishop—Lieutenant Colonel William Avery Bishop, V.C., the Canadian ace—with his record of having bagged, officially, seventy-two German planes.

I am not sure that I would not be justified in dubbing him ace of aces, the greatest war flyer of them all. After studying the birds of prey, he chose the methods of the hawk. He was a human hawk, cool, calculating, swift.

He was lone like the hawk, a supreme solo fighter. He cruised alone. He killed alone. He led patrols, of course, but even then managed to detach himself. Most of the time he went up by himself and ranged free lance, his keen eyes seeking prey.

Besides these methods, he possessed that subtle thing which makes champions in any game of combat—intuitive skill, which is a natural gift, flowering with experience.

A friend of mine, observing one day in a two-seater near Lens, recognized Bishop's flight 3,000 feet above. At the

9

same time, slightly south, he noticed a formation of Germans.

"Now I'll see something!" he thought and his glance ranged the sky. He watched—but nothing happened. Bishop just kept cruising around.

" 'S funny!"

He knew that if he could see the enemy it was a sure bet that Bishop's famed eyes had long since picked them out.

Still nothing happened. He kept watching, wondering, for a full fifteen minutes. Then, his heart jumped. For, like bass darting in a pool, Bishop and his flight wheeled and dived downwind.

They caught the Germans as they lost speed on a turn. The timing was perfect.

Biff! Bang! Two of the enemy planes pitched out of control. Bishop got one. A fellow pilot got the other.

Just an ordinary incident of Bishop's career, but nothing could illustrate better the cool sureness of his thrust. To my mind the war produced no greater ace. It will be argued, of course, that as against his seventy-two planes Richthofen, the Red Knight of Germany, was credited with eighty. True, and I have no wish to try to hurt the glory of that great enemy pilot. But he was different from Bishop in his methods and his results.

The baron seldom flew or fought except in formation. He was a hide hunter. He picked off lame ducks pulling from a fight. He specialized in swooping on slow-motion artillery planes. In the mornings he had the advantage of the sun, when it showed, behind him as he lay in wait for enemies. The prevailing west wind was to his advantage in getting home from a scrap.

It is significant that he knew the names of most of the pilots he brought down, because most of his fights were over home territory.

His total was augmented by planes which he drove down without destroying.

If Bishop had been similarly credited with machines driven down but not destroyed, his total would have been well over a hundred. But the British system allowed only claims for planes crashed or sent down in flames and these only when verified by other observers. Since ninety per cent of his fights were over enemy country Bishop could not follow and claim machines forced to land unhurt.

Unlike Richthofen, Bishop knew the name of scarcely a man he downed. The pilots he killed were impersonal enemies.

Strange that it should have been so, since he was, by instinct and reason, an individualist. He sought to fight on his own terms—and they were bold ones. His precise tactics, evolved by intelligent planning and a cold, almost mathematical fightcraft, were dependent on solo effort.

An analysis of his fights, and he had more than 200, shows that seventy-five per cent of them were undertaken alone, and, in the main, against odds. He picked off slow planes, of course, since his job was to destroy the enemy and since he made no secret of the fact that he was out to pile up a score. But mostly he pitted his skill against the fastest scouts. He attacked them singly. He smashed into groups.

Fast, terrible, his guns blazing, he crashed into formations of as many as nine and by sheer *élan* frequently sent down one or two.

Bishop's last war day in France will illustrate. It was a day of individual glory such as few other airmen achieved.

But I offer Bishop's bag that day as a record for a single flight. He got five in less than two hours, four of them new-type scouts. And he got them alone. When he set out that morning his score was sixty-seven. Before lunch it had risen to seventy-two. It was his grand finale.

That was on a June day, 1918, back of Ypres. Ordered to report back to England for administrative duty, with every possible honor an airman could gain, he had gone out alone seeking one last thrill. He got it.

The gods were good. He had scarcely crossed the lines, high in the clouds, when his keen eyes marked three Pfalz scouts, a new, fast German type. No odds here, but his regular meat.

He dived on the nearest. His guns ripped out one of those short, close bursts which were his specialty and the enemy ship fell flaming in a spin.

Hearing the rattle of his guns, the remaining pair swung

over and at him. And two other scouts, out of a layer above, came diving down on him.

But let Bishop's official report tell the rest of the story:

> The second and third of the enemy scouts circled around me, trying to get under my tail, and as I dived beneath them they collided and fell together, the first bursting into flames. The remaining two started to climb away, and I chased them, opening fire at two hundred yards. One of them went into an uncontrollable spin and crashed. The other zoomed into the clouds and escaped.

Four out of five fast scouts wiped out by a lone Canadian in ten minutes!

It is typical of Bishop that he was not satisfied. Whetted, he kept on cruising beyond the lines. His report continues:

> Near Neuve Église I met a two-seater which I attacked from behind and beneath. It burst into flames and crashed. Zooming down to see what happened I encountered a column of enemy troops on the march and scattered them. Then I climbed into the clouds and went home.

That was his last act of active war. On this fourth trip to France, in May and June, 1918, he had destroyed twenty-five planes in twelve days, including the five just mentioned. For all this he was given the Distinguished Flying Cross.

In 1916 Bishop had spent four months at the front as an observer without tasting blood. When he returned to England to become a pilot he had not been under fire.

Before he could start training he had to spend months in hospital with a knee hurt when a pilot crashed. It was his only wound. Thousands of tracers subsequently sought him. He came back to the base with as many as fifty bullets in his plane—with his engine shot up, holes in his tank, his wings riven. And once a bullet ripped his cap. But never once was he hit himself.

Toward the end of '16, having qualified as a pilot, he served as a Zeppelin hunter in England, but never saw a dirigible. Thus, when he went to France to a fighting squadron in the early spring of '17, it was with a suppressed, almost virginal urge to prove his mettle. He proved it, with speed. In less than two months' fighting he won the Military Cross, the Distinguished Service Order and, Britain's supreme reward for valor, the Victoria Cross.

Bishop's first fight was on March 25, 1917.

In the next two weeks he had half a dozen scraps, just missed being taken prisoner, and got his first three Huns.

Then on April 7 he won the Military Cross. The official statement of the award gave as reason:

> For conspicuous gallantry and devotion to duty. He attacked a hostile balloon on the ground, dispersed the crew and destroyed the balloon, and also drove down a hostile machine which attacked him. He has on several occasions brought down hostile machines.

This bleak statement does not say that he was again within a few feet of being taken prisoner. His solo escapade took place five miles within the enemy lines. Just as he set himself to dive on the balloon from 5,000 feet, he was attacked by a single-seater. Bullets cut through his wings. He immelmanned and raked the enemy as he shot past. As he fell, Bishop dived after him, to make sure.

Then he swooped after the balloon until he was within fifty feet of the ground. His tracers tore through its sides, firing it. But as he machine-gunned the crew, his engine failed. He had picked out a tree on which to smash his plane when, unexpectedly, the motor started—and he hedge-hopped, through gunfire, home.

Less than four weeks later, on May 2, he won the D.S.O. Again let me quote the official award:

> For conspicuous gallantry and devotion to duty. While in a single-seater he attacked three hostile machines, two of which he brought down, although in the meantime he was himself attacked by other hostile machines. His courage and determination have set a fine example to others.

Sounds simple as signing a check!

Facts were, Bishop, flying alone, had come on three two-seaters, artillery observing. He dived. They scurried, zigzagging. Picking one, he swept to within twenty yards and slung a short drag. The pilot slumped. The plane crashed.

Meantime its two fellows were climbing toward him; and out of the clouds above came four scouts, two firing as they came.

He seemed sandwiched.

But invariably, when crowded, Bishop played a bold hand. Swinging past the nearest two-seater, he spewed a burst into its side and shot it down. Then he turned his nose up to the four oncoming scouts. Straight as a dart he went at one, head on, firing. It was a bold move he had made again and again. The German gave way first. Bishop went into a spinning nose dive and fell hundreds of feet. Then he pulled out and flew home.

On May 10 he went to England on two weeks' leave. He wanted to stay at the front and fight and fight. He never felt happier. But he went—and ten days after his return he won the Victoria Cross.

At that time his record was twenty-two. He wanted to bring his bag up. So he conceived and planned an attack on an enemy airdrome, picking June 2 for the raid.

That morning he had himself called at three o'clock. It was still night as he dressed and went out toward the hangars without breakfast. No one knew of his plan but a couple of friends. And they thought him crazy.

That did not worry him. He carried through, and before he returned for breakfast he had pulled off one of the most daring individual exploits of the war. From the official citation and other reports it is possible to reconstruct that cold-nerved thrust at dawn.

Picture Bishop in a one-gun Nieuport single-seater setting off from the sleeping base near Vimy Ridge and climbing by the first faint light on his lonely adventure. There was a ground mist. The air was chill. The world seemed dead. Even the war seemed done. He shivered.

But he swung out toward an airdrome he had marked.

Picture him growing more tense as he drew near. Imagine,

then, his disappointment. The drome was deserted. Not a plane was to be seen.

Did he turn back, glad of the excuse? No, that would not have been Bishop. He set his mouth harder and went farther. And shortly he sighted the hangars and huts of another drome. Ah, this was better! Meat, on ice!

He dropped to 500 feet, pulled up, circled. Seven machines. Six scouts and a two-seater, their engines running. Good. He ought to get four, at least.

Men came rushing across the drome with machine guns. Pilots climbed into the planes.

Above them Bishop poised, a boy with fair hair and a little blond mustache in a plane. Then, suddenly, he struck.

Sticking his nose down, he dived and swept the ground with his gun. A man fell. He zoomed and watched again. One of the scouts left the ground. He turned, swept on its tail, and fired. It crashed. He swung up and around.

A second scout took off. He did not wait now. He flew over it, firing. It crumpled against a tree.

Two more machines were now off the ground. He climbed. One of them followed. He immelmanned, circled, dived from 1,000 feet. Into it he ripped the last bullets of his last drum and caught it with his last shot. It fell outside the drome.

Three up! In ten minutes' fighting! And an airdrome all torn up. Good again.

Bishop had hoped for four, but there was no chance. He had no ammunition. He had to get out and away. His plane had holes in it. Machine guns still sprayed him from the ground. His head suddenly turned dizzy. His stomach, without food, felt empty and queer. Near by in the air was an enemy and about 1,000 feet above his keen eyes sighted four German scouts.

So he wheeled out for home and made it. The enemy were content to hover over him, though he was defenseless, which they did not know.

His exploit was confirmed, most particularly since a Victoria Cross was involved. Captured airmen told what he'd done. It had been the talk of the German flying forces.

In August, 1917, Bishop returned, on orders, to England to be attached to the School of Aircraft Gunnery, but before he went he added a bar to his D.S.O., which was equivalent to a second award.

He had been in France five months. In that time he had cleaned up Britain's roster of fighting decorations, except the Distinguished Flying Cross, which he won in 1918. He had destroyed forty-seven enemy machines officially and driven down twenty-three which he could not claim. He had been in 110 fights.

This Canadian of twenty-three had scaled war's pinnacle. He had become almost a legend. His tactics, his machine gunnery, his dash, his lone hawk fights, his cool impassivity, his superb disdain, his apparent invincibility had made him a veritable demigod. Even the smothering methods of the British censor could not hide his flame.

Already he was Bishop the nonpareil. His short month's return to France in 1918, when in twelve days he got twenty-five more planes, added to his score but merely gave an extra frill to his reputation. By now his dash was rated. His chest blazed with ribbons like a field marshal's.

Like Richthofen, Bishop was originally a cavalry officer. As a lad from Orillia, Ontario, he had attended the Royal Military College at Kingston, Canada's West Point. Shortly after the war broke out he went overseas as a subaltern in the Missisauga Horse. He loved horses. But, training in England in the mud, as he relates it, his imagination was caught one day by the flashing ease of a plane. He entered the Royal Flying Corps.

Bishop was not the only Canadian to win fame as a pilot, for thousands of his young countrymen flocked to the air like ducks to a pond, forming toward the end of the war almost half the personnel of the British flying services.

Canada produced four flyers whose aggregate score was not beaten, so far as I know: Billy Bishop, V.C., Bill Barker, V.C., Ray Collishaw, who was recommended for the V.C., and Don McLaren. Among them they won enough other decorations to load a wheelbarrow.

These men destroyed by exact official count 230 enemy machines: Bishop, seventy-two; Collishaw, sixty; Barker, fifty; and McLaren, forty-eight. The war's Big Four!

Every one of them returned from the front, although poor Barker, hero of a single-handed fight with sixty enemy machines in which he won the V.C. but lost an arm, was to die a few months ago in a peacetime flip near Ottawa.

Britain had gallant stars like Ball, Mannock, McCudden, V.C. winners who were killed when their scores were around fifty, but no British four quite touched these Canadians' total. Nor did any French four. Guynemer, top man, had fifty-three. The brilliant Fonck was below that. So was Nungesser.

As for Germany's biggest four, Richthofen had eighty and Udet had sixty-two, but none of the others, so far as I can learn, had over forty. The highest possible score of Richthofen, Udet, and any two other German aces would be 222.

By the way, it is worth recording that in March, 1928, Colonel Bishop was the guest in Berlin of a number of German aces and, proposed by Udet, was made a member of the German Ace Association; and that three months later, in London, he was in turn dinner host to eight leading German flyers.

And now let us analyze the reasons for Bishop's supremacy. First of all, he had remarkable eyes, telescopic eyes, the eyes of a questing falcon. Men who flew with him on patrol say that he would signal enemy aircraft from three to five minutes before the other pilots could pick them out. The faintest speck, half hidden by a distant cloud, was not too small for his long-range eyes to register.

This gave him an overwhelming advantage in this war of the air in which position and surprise were nine points toward victory.

Because of his eyes he was off on a long, high climb into the sun or stealthily skirting the edge of the heavens toward a favorable point from which to strike long before the enemy were aware of him. Or he was working in behind to come up on their blind beam from below.

Many a Heinie only learned of his presence when his guns spoke, and then, often, too late. For one out of, roughly, four German planes which faced him went down.

In Winged Warfare, his own story of his 1917 campaign, he placed in the order of their value: first machine gunnery; second, tactics; and third, flying ability.

I have already touched on his tactics. He was a master of

sky ringcraft. He timed his punch like a champion boxer. Having won his position, or at the least sign of weak strategy, he tore into an opponent and finished him, as often as not, in the first round.

That brings us to his gunnery.

He scarcely ever fired at long range. His specialty was infighting. He seldom fired until the enemy was a mere length or two, twenty, thirty, at the most fifty yards away. He waited until he had a bead on his opponent's vitals. Then he snapped out a short, sharp drag.

It is amazing the number of times he dropped an enemy with his first burst of a few rounds.

His tracers blazed straight because he made himself a master of machine gunnery. His eyes helped here, too. He was, with the possible exception of Fonck, the air's greatest sharpshooter. To begin with, he never took his guns for granted, like many pilots. He got to know them like a gunnery sergeant. Several times when they jammed in a scrap he pulled out, flipped around, fixed them, and then darted in again to finish up an opponent.

With his intimate mechanical knowledge went a shooting accuracy which few approached. He practiced with his guns until he won a skill that was almost automatic.

He spent hours at the base diving at a target, especially if he returned from a mishit flight.

One of his greatest assets, in maneuvering and shooting, was his patience. He built up his self-control until it became an unassailable ally.

One day, he relates in his book, he saw a solitary scout at a great height. Climbing carefully, he got between it and the sun and waited. He waited, cool as a poised hawk, until the enemy made a favorable turn. Then he dived, hard, and slipped under his tail without being seen. Withholding his fire, he crept up until he could see the markings of the unsuspecting Boche.

His eyes ranged along his sights. His thumb lay on the button. Yet closer he crept until he was less than twenty yards behind and beneath. Then, precisely as a surgeon selecting a place to cut, he picked the exact spot to hit, right below the unseen pilot.

Only then did he fire sharply—just twenty rounds.

He saw them rip into the bottom of the fuselage.

His enemy lurched, then plunged. Bishop had to side-slip off, so close was he to the path of the falling plane. A few feet down, and the enemy ship burst into flame.

So you have the picture of him as a stalker and shot. He was dispassionate as an Indian on the trail. To him this was big-game hunting, and the fact that human lives were involved was submerged. "Great sport," he called it in a letter home. "I never enjoyed myself so much in my life." That was in the early days. The only change later was a greater coolness, a subtler finesse, a more serious application to achieve.

It became then an ambition, rather than a sport. In Winged Warfare he once wrote, "I began to feel as if my list of victims was not climbing as steadily as I would have liked. . . . So I went over the lines from six to seven hours every day, praying for some easy victim to appear. I had had some pretty hard fighting. Now I wanted to shoot a 'rabbit' or two."

To his glory, though, it may be said that the majority of those with whom he tilted were fast fighting scouts and he often gave them odds of four, five, and six to one.

"To bring down a machine," he wrote in another place, "did not seem like killing a man. It was more as if one had just destroyed a mechanical target with no human being in it . . . very much as if one was shooting down clay pigeons."

How great was his control, how sure were his tactics, how calm was his judgment, may be gauged from the fact that from the middle of May, 1917, until he left France in August he lost only one man killed out of his patrol. And that man was shot on a flight in which he did not participate.

Bishop was controlled always. You could not imagine him whooping, as many pilots did through sheer strain, when they shot down a plane. Being a precisionist, he did not shout when he plugged an enemy machine, any more than Bobby Jones would sinking a putt.

On the ground he was equally self-contained. Aces like Barker and Collishaw were idols. Their fellows felt kinship. But Bishop was austere, aloof, godlike.

Even flying, he was not a stunter, not a grand-stander. He kept his feelings corked. Many men used to celebrate a kill by split-essing all over the home drome. He never did. He would slip in, turn his bus over to his mechanics, designate overhaul or repairs, and hike off to tennis.

Yet he might have just come from a scrap that would have left an ordinary man twittering.

For he had many narrow escapes. Indeed, his career might have ended on his very first fight, when he had to land with a dead engine. But fortunately he found he had glided within British lines with a hundred yards to spare.

Not only did Bishop destroy seventy-two planes, but several balloons. But this was too much like potting tame ducks to satisfy his combat instincts. He only did it under orders, and then thoroughly. He did get a kick, however, out of raking enemy trenches and diving on masses of troops. That appealed to his sense of sport.

A detailed account of his flights and fights during his aggregate of six months' service would crowd columns. He was seldom out of the air when flying was feasible. He flew as many as eight hours a day. During a single hour he once engaged, single-handed, eleven different planes. Like a flashing devil, he wheeled out of one scrap into another. During this particular hour, he crashed one, drove down another, forced half a dozen two-seaters to quit artillery observation, and kept five scouts from harassing British artillery observers.

His speed of execution was terrific. His shifting was fast as lightning. And his guns spoke like a thunderbolt. It was not out of the way for him to get two planes out of four —Brrp! Brrp! One! Two!—with almost a continuous burst on the same dive.

He seldom went out without finding adventure, although he did not always score. One day he exchanged shots three times with Richthofen's circus without result. That was on the morning of April 30, 1917, when he had nine separate fights over German territory in back of Lens and Monchy between nine forty-five and twelve fifteen. The first was on patrol, the others on his own.

He was flying a Nieuport scout armed with a single Lewis gun. Included was an engagement with two three-seater

Gothas. Later he crashed one of three artillery two-seaters. Then, three times he mixed it with the five red Halberstadt scouts, harassing them until he forced them to land.

That same afternoon, accompanied by a second plane, he engaged four red scouts which he believed included Richthofen. It was a merry fracas. The six fast machines, flown by cracks, circled and dashed, dived and zoomed, immelmanned and flipped in a battle royal. Bishop fired two bursts of five rounds at the leader, presumably Richthofen, without result. He fired ten at another plane. There was no chance for accurate aim. This was pinch-hit scrapping. Bullets struck within an inch of his own head.

It would have been epic if Bishop had got Richthofen, or vice versa, but four strange planes all of a sudden came butting in. Both sides paused; pulled out to look. They proved to be British naval triplanes. The Germans disappeared.

A couple of days later Bishop had seven more individual tilts without a kill. And the day following, when he was cruising along, half asleep, a Boche came at him suddenly out of the sun. But his luck held. He flipped over on the first burst and dived.

He had his off days, but fortune always rode with him, even when he missed.

After winning the Victoria Cross, before leaving France in August, 1917, as a gloriously arisen ace, Bishop continued to fight with verve. He grew superb in his mastery of this game of sudden death. Each victory added to his assurance. When he could not shoot down enemies he bluffed them. One day, scrapping with three planes, he used up his ammunition and pulled out—just as the Huns, as if by common consent, did likewise. They came back. So did he, with empty drums, and went right at them. And they quit. It was during this period that he added the bar to his D.S.O.

He has destroyed (said the official citation) no fewer than forty-five machines in the past five months, frequently attacking enemy formations single-handed, and on all occasions displaying a fighting spirit and determination to get to close quarters with his opponents, which have earned the admiration of all in contact with him.

After his long interlude in England from August, 1917, to May, 1918, he returned to France with this spirit and determination on edge, and in little more than a month at the front soared to Olympian heights. It was during twelve flying days of this period that he got twenty-five planes, the last five on his final day. He was now indeed Bishop the unconquerable.

On his very first day back, mixing it with a two-seater, he was attacked by ten enemy scouts. Climbing right through them, firing, he managed to escape in a cloud. He kept on climbing and at 17,000 feet tackled a two-seater, which he smashed over Passchendaele. His eye was in.

The day following, near Thourout, he found himself above nine German scouts. Without counting the odds, he dived, clipped one with a thirty-round burst, and saw it fall flaming.

His falcon thrust had scattered the flock.

He kept on diving through them. Six hundred feet below his first kill, he twisted, spat out another burst, and dropped a second plane blazing.

Five minutes of hell fire, then off and away! That was Bishop on his return to the front.

Wet days intervened. Next time up, east of Hazebrouck, he knocked a two-seater to bits in the air. That afternoon he scrimmaged around the edge of a patrol of fourteen slow ones, convoyed by fast scouts. He darted in, flung a drag or two at the nearest machines, but failed to score. Having thrown the formation out, he scooted.

An hour later he drove down an artillery machine which landed and did not count.

Another day, still solo, he sought change up on the coast by Nieuport and Ostend. Sighting eight Albatros scouts, he waited, poised in his well known way above and behind, biding the time to strike. It came. One straggled. He dived. It fell in flames into the North Sea.

Zooming to a convenient cloud, he watched for a second chance as the disorganized Huns cut circles seeking him. It came, too. He swooped. And a second plane went down in flames. Then he popped back into the clouds and vanished. Elusive as a phantom.

June had come before he flew again. Then one day he and his patrol mixed it with six scouts. They bagged four. Bishop got the leader. The others fell to his patrol. Thus he destroyed the enemy. I am only touching at random on a few high spots of those twelve days of inspired flying. Once, over Roulers, intent on weighing his chances if he went after some enemy scouts high up and miles away, he was attacked without warning by three two-seaters.

He dropped for his life—so low that he was machine-gunned from the ground. But he zigzagged over the trenches, then all of a sudden zoomed—and caught the nearest Boche with a fifty-round burst. The enemy crashed, burning.

The remaining pair came at him and he had the unusual experience of a tail-chasing merry-go-round. At last, though, he got one dead on his sights and fired. It fell out of control and crashed.

The third made off. He followed, and chased it fifty miles without catching up. It escaped finally in a cloud.

On his way home he fought two Albatros scouts. He drove one down out of control beside the German trenches, where it was pounded to bits by British guns. He sent the second down in a spin, but was "archied" too heavily to make sure it crashed, and therefore could not claim it.

Three planes on one flight! Thus he brought up his bag.

On another occasion near Armentières he had just crashed a two-seater at 8,000 feet when four Albatros scouts came down at him out of the sun. He was not aware of them until he heard the rrrp! of their guns. With him action was fast as thought. He fell spinning 4,000 feet, flattened, then climbed full speed into the sun. It was his turn now and he did not miss.

He dived at the nearest, so straight indeed that a collision was averted only by his shooting. At seventy-five yards a burst sent his enemy slipping to a crash—and he slid past where he had been a moment before.

Before he could fight further, a British patrol scared off the other three.

Once in a gap in the clouds he came on four scouts lying in ambush. He barged into them and with his first drag hit an enemy's gas tank. There was an explosion and the plane fell in flames. Banking at an awkward angle, he got another on his sights and fired, peculiarly enough causing another explosion. And a second machine fell flaming. The two left scurried off in the clouds.

As a climax to all this came that last great day, of which I have already told, when he bumped off five planes as a man might smash clay pigeons at a shooting meet.

All he got for this Homeric flying was the Distinguished Flying Cross. Britain had nothing else to give, short of a peerage.

Thus ended Bishop's great adventure as a winged warrior. He was made a lieutenant colonel and brought back to England in June, 1918. Evidently the authorities wanted to preserve his flying genius to help train fighting pilots for the last intensive months of the war.

There is little more to be told. After the war he came back for a time to Canada and with Colonel William Barker, V.C., his great Canadian rival for premier honors, launched a venture in commercial flying which was no doubt born too soon. It died, and Bishop returned to England.

But just as the war gave him fame, so as a sequel, it gave him fortune.

He joined with a young engineer in a scheme which involved the reclaiming of material from the British military dumps in France. It is said the two young men made millions. Then he turned to banking and finance. He is said to have added to his fortune.

He has stayed in England. He lives in Regent's Park. He breeds chow dogs. He plays polo at Hurlingham. He rides to hounds with the Bucks. He belongs to the Bath Club. He is a solid British citizen of the better class.

The hawk has clipped his wings.

Flying to Kill

BY ALAN HYND

◎ ◎ ◎ ◎ ◎ ◎ ◎ ◎ ◎

PART ONE—AN ACE IS BORN

WHEN the hoofbeats of the Four Horsemen of the Apocalypse resounded across the seas last September, the eyes of the Dominion of Canada turned to a handful of men. One of these men was Billy Bishop—or, rather, Lieutenant Colonel William Avery Bishop, Victoria Cross, Distinguished Service Order and Bar, Military Cross, Distinguished Flying Cross, Chevalier of the Legion of Honor, Croix de Guerre with Palm. Then, out of the semi-obscurity of private life, a smiling blond almost legendary figure was plucked by the Minister of National Defense to be the Honorary Marshal of the Royal Canadian Air Force, and hearts beat faster from Quebec to Vancouver, from Toronto to the Hudson Strait.

"Bishop flies again!" was the phrase that echoed throughout the Dominion. A great country girding for the ordeal of wiping Hitlerism from the earth was speaking of the man who, in the opinion of numerous impartial historians of the last World War, was the colossus of the skies. Here had been a boy who, just turned twenty, had enlisted in the cavalry, gotten himself transferred to the Royal Flying Corps, and in an incredibly short time participated in upward of two hundred major air battles. His official record is seventy-two planes shot down, but the unofficial though nonetheless certain fact is that Bishop sent well over a hundred enemy sky fighters to their doom.

25

What an inspiration, then, today, to young Canadian manhood is this handsome man of forty-five, of medium height, with taffy-colored hair and closely cropped mustache, and with eyes that match his light blue marshal's uniform! Yes, only forty-five, and in that tanned face not a single trace of the inferno of a quarter of a century ago, when he flew, sometimes ten hours a day, to kill—or be killed.

A fabulous huntsman of the blue who fought to the death; who gave no quarter, and who asked none; who surrendered himself to the furies and shot down twenty-five enemy craft in ten days.

A twentieth-century knight who knew his greatest fear when, in Buckingham Palace, he walked toward the King to receive the Victoria Cross and heard his boots squeak. That was Billy Bishop!

In his study in the Laurentian Hills on the outskirts of Montreal there is a bullet-punctured windscreen from the warplane of the White Knight of Canada. Another knight put the puncture there—Baron Manfred von Richthofen, the Red Knight of Germany. There were two historic duels between these two, whose lives strangely paralleled each other, except that Bishop lives to fly again while Richthofen looks on from Valhalla. A piece of Richthofen's plane—the color of blood—hangs in the Bishop study, too. "He was a great fighter—and a gentleman," says the Marshal.

Today Billy Bishop, as he is affectionately called in the news rooms of the great Canadian dailies, is up there at the back door of heaven for a good percentage of hours out of each twenty-four; not stalking, maneuvering, and diving, now, with his right index finger on a Lewis gun's lever, but en route to the key points of the Dominion where the youths of the Royal Canadian Air Force—"my baby"—are being taught the art of aerial combat.

Each boy in the Canadian corps is going to have a real bag of aerial tricks as part of his equipment before he looks upon the second western front. Bishop will see to that. Too many of his young friends twenty-odd years ago went down in flames. "Replacements of men and planes were coming up to the front so fast," the Marshal told me, when Liberty sent me to the Dominion to get the story of the White Knight at first hand, "that the boys frequently didn't have the opportunity to get the feel of their ships and, in consequence, were often shot down the first hour. That won't happen again!"

The man who was one day to be feared by every enemy on the western front—except Richthofen—was born in Owen Sound, a peaceful and deeply religious little community in the lake and hill country of Ontario. Bishop's roots went back to England on both his father's and mother's sides. His dad was a prosperous lawyer. There were lawyers, statesmen, engineers, and architects—and soldiers—in the family tree.

He was a thoroughly normal boy, perhaps a little more given to devil-raising than the average kid. He had one brother, Worth, ten years his senior, and a younger sister. Worth was studying to be an engineer; but Billy at the age of ten, attending public school in Owen Sound, hadn't the faintest idea as to what he wanted to be. He did have a somewhat restless nature, and never particularly distinguished himself in the classroom. When he polished off his homework in a hurry, that merely meant that he wanted to join the "gang" early enough to get in some doorbell ringing before bedtime.

It was when Billy was ten that he first laid eyes on quite the prettiest girl he had ever seen. He announced to his amused parents that he was going to marry her some day. She was a picture in white organdy, with laughing dark eyes and raven hair. Her name was Margaret Eaton Burden, and she was the granddaughter of the Canadian department-store magnate, Timothy Eaton. Miss Burden was five, going on six.

With her family, she came up summers from Toronto to Georgian Bay, on which Owen Sound is situated. Billy was an outdoor boy, and he used to point out to her gaily colored birds that a little girl never saw in the city. She talked about him so much that the two families eventually became acquainted. Fall came, and she went away. But she didn't forget, and neither did Billy.

When he was twelve, he entered Owen Sound Collegiate, which took youths from his age up to seventeen to fit them for the Royal Military College at Kingston, Ontario. He saw quite a bit of little Miss Burden again during the summer. She was going on eight now, and had a mind of her own. She knew that Billy Bishop was going to be her hero forever and ever.

At seventeen Billy entered Royal Military College. His father thought the boy might take up civil engineering. Although on the slight side physically, he played baseball, football, and basketball, and was a fearless horseman. It was at this time, too, that he went in for hunting. He was a crack shot, and he had a pair of eyes that could, naked, see distant objects discernible to other eyes only through field glasses.

Billy never cared for girls—except one, the little girl of the white organdy. She was now growing into quite a young lady, and whenever he could he would visit her parents' home in Toronto.

Truth to tell, he wasn't so much as undecided as to what his future would be after his first year at R.M.C. He hadn't even thought about it. In his second year, though, civil engineering began to cross his mind. He couldn't imagine being a prisoner in an office. There was adventure—and danger—in engineering.

His adventurous spirit was coming into full flower as 1914 dawned. Then, just when he had completed his third year at R.M.C., the Four Horsemen thundered over Europe. Canada went to the colors when Germany's Kaiser plunged the civilized world into a nightmare.

Margaret Burden was worried. What girl wouldn't have been? But she smiled bravely during Billy's first visit to the great house at 494 Avenue Road, Toronto, after the Dominion had declared war on Germany. "Of course you're going to enlist, Billy," she said quietly. "I would expect it of you—and I know it's what you want to do anyway. I just pray that the war will not last too long."

The recruiting officer glanced twice at the twenty-year-old Bishop when Billy walked in and asked to be taken into "whatever outfit is going over first." Not so much his fighting blood as his sporting blood was aroused. Danger of all sorts; the challenge to the huntsman.

He got in all right, as a lieutenant in the Missisauga Horse of Toronto. One night, months after he had enlisted, he called at the home on Avenue Road. A sleet storm was pounding Toronto. It was January, 1915. He left a ring that night. Margaret Burden had promised to become Mrs. William Avery Bishop—some day. The Missisauga Horse were sailing on the morrow.

The boys had a fifteen-day trip over that was malodorous if uneventful. Six hundred and ninety-odd of the seven hundred horses aboard got seasick. Then England, and more training camps, and mud, mud, mud. Mud up to Billy Bishop's ankles and sometimes halfway to his knees. The lads came down with flu, and a lot of them dropped off like flies. And not even in France yet! Would they never get to the front?

One day the young lieutenant gazed wistfully at a trim little Royal Flying Corps scouting plane that soared into the gray mists above the training camp. Suddenly he came to a momentous decision. He determined to apply for transfer to the Royal Flying Corps. What difference did it make that he had never even been up in an airplane? It wasn't, in fact, flying itself that caused him to decide; it was just that flying represented the most complete escape from a life of being bogged down and made helpless in mud and slime.

Bishop had a long row to hoe before he was to fulfill his dream of solo exploit in the skies. He had, as he says, the stomach for flying—that is, just sitting in the back, observing, with some one else at the stick. The very first time he ever left the ground, he knew the sky was his destiny. It was love at first flight. An old training bus that couldn't make much more than fifty miles an hour, and which, when climbing, shook and rattled like a slow freight on a tough grade, was where the Canadian youth won his first insignia of the Royal Flying Corps—an O with one outstretched wing attached, which meant he was a full-fledged observer.

Reconnaissance work entailed enormous risk and no glory. On his first flight over German territory as an observer, Bishop got his first bird's-eye view of the war. He had photographs of enemy terrain, taken the day before, and it was up to him to look down and see that everything was still as it had been. Back of the lines, the artillery was preparing to smash spots in the subjects of those pictures.

Other British machines that set out at the same time—just after dawn—were doing bombing, artillery, and photographic work. The young man from Owen Sound thrilled as he looked back over his own lines and saw the big long-range guns talking crimson language.

The new observer was up more than an hour that first time.

The crate he was in rolled around. The going was rough. And the "Archies" in the German lines weren't making things any better as they sent up exploding shells and black shrapnel puffballs. The pilot could see the puffballs coming, and therefore had one chance in ten of getting out of the way if the aim was good. It was pretty good once, for a ball all but lifted Billy Bishop and his maps right out of the back seat.

The pilot kept looking back at him and grinning—no use trying to talk—and when they came in, he shook hands with him. "Congratulations, lieutenant," he said. "You didn't get the wind up." They called the jitters, or worse, getting the wind up.

In the months that followed, Lieutenant Bishop did bombing and artillery work. He began to get himself talked about. He never got the wind up. He was known as the man without nerves. But he grew moody and dissatisfied. This business of sitting in the back seat while somebody else handled the stick wasn't up his alley. There was no sport in dropping a few hundred pounds of explosives on chaps who didn't have a chance to defend themselves. It was too easy. It lacked challenge. There was nothing of the hunt about it. But take a job in one of those trim little scouting planes that got into wing-to-wing duels—well, *that* was really something that would test a man's mettle.

He had plenty of chance to lay his plans to get through the red tape of promotion. His pilot inadvertently saw to that. The ship was landing one day when it struck something rough, and Billy Bishop's knee was reduced to pulp. He astonished everybody by insisting upon limping around on a crutch, and eventually wound up in a hospital for many maddening months. That was in the spring of 1916. He wrote to Margaret Burden of his impatience to get well and take up soloing.

When the smashed knee was mended, Bishop got the good news. His superiors had been thinking things over. A man so immune to getting the wind up should make a good solo flyer!

Truth to tell, he got off to anything but an auspicious start, and his letters to Miss Burden at this time were anything but encouraging. He told her that he was "ham-handed"—

gripped the stick too tightly. Then he went to the other extreme—grew timid-handed.

But he was a glutton for work—and flying was his work. At length he was permitted to make his first flight behind the lines. It was passable. More training flights followed, and one day he was given two wings to wear over his left breast. Now he was a full-fledged member of the Royal Flying Corps. Whereupon he was sent from France to London, to guard the mouth of the Thames. He wrote Miss Burden that the inactivity there palled on him.

The youth from Ontario wanted to get to the front. In February, 1917, Baron Manfred von Richthofen, the Kaiser's deadliest ace, had bagged twenty-five enemy ships, and Bishop wanted to get into action like that. And so, on March 7, when he was twenty-three, he landed at Boulogne, France, and joined Squadron Sixty of the Royal Flying Corps.

Captain Albert Ball, reigning ace of the R.F.C., was attached to Squadron Sixty, and forthwith became Bishop's hero. Alongside of Ball's name on the Headquarters blackboard was the figure 29, far and away the highest score of any aviator behind the Allied lines.

A dark, handsome, and strange young figure was Captain Ball. He seemed obsessed with the idea of killing as many Germans as possible. He was moody and at times antisocial. He would retire to his quarters and play a phonograph. Not jazz stuff. Beethoven and the other music masters. Whenever possible, he had his room filled with freshly cut flowers. The flowers and the music inspired him—to map plans for the morrow's kill.

It was Ball who told Bishop about Richthofen's Flying Circus; of how the Head Hunters—members of that scarlet-shipped Circus, usually five or six in number—used to delight in hiding in the clouds and pouncing on an Allied lame duck. Billy Bishop's teeth clenched hard on the stem of his pipe when Ball told him about that five-to-one business. "I won't be flying entirely for sport now," he said. "I'll be *flying to kill*, too."

"Yes," said Ball. "You've got to get them—or they'll get you. It's that simple."

The brand-new French single-seater Nieuport scouts, the Allies' answer to the German Albatros, were coming up right then, and Bishop got one of them. It wasn't as big or fast as the Albatros, but it was capable of quicker maneuvering. A Lewis gun, fitted above the upper plane, fired over the propeller. The sights were directly in front of the pilot's head, so that he could take aim without changing his position in the seat. To fire, all he had to do was to press a lever on the control stick.

Bishop's first patrol was almost his last. He went out with five others, bringing up the rear. He knew right then that he wasn't cut out for formation flying. He was either right on the tail of the ship in front of him, or lagging far behind. Then he became fascinated by the panorama below him, and when he looked up again the five ships supposed to be in front of him weren't there. They had made a left-hand turn and were almost a mile off, and far to the rear.

He turned and streaked for them. He noticed that, as he did so, they turned as if to come back for him, then resumed their original course. Back at the airdrome, Ball said to him, "The Head Hunters almost got you. Five of them were coming down from the top side of some fluff. They thought you were a loner—then they saw the rest of the patrol turning around and they beat it."

In the middle of March, 1917, the Germans were retreating from the Somme and falling back on the Hindenburg Line. Bishop was preparing for his first life-and-death struggle. A fast friendship was growing between the maestro of the skies and the fledgling, and Ball used to take Bishop into his quarters at night and draw diagrams for him, showing which way to move when trapped, just like a football coach mapping strategy. One of Ball's favorite stunts when greatly outnumbered was to stick so close to the tail of one particular enemy machine that the rest would withhold their fire for fear of downing their comrade. Then, the moment another of the pursuing machines became separated from the rest, the Englishman would pour lead into the craft immediately ahead of him, then go after that other and repeat the performance until he saw a chance for another kill, or for escape. The result of all this was that Billy Bishop could do just about everything except make that Nieuport of his talk by March 25—the day of his first battle.

The German retreat is well under way, and the fixed

battle lines have all but vanished. Bishop and two other men from Squadron Sixty go out under a low ceiling in the afternoon with instructions to proceed beyond the German lines to serve as a forward wall for some reconnaissance ships. Just about where the enemy line begins to take form, the weather clears, and the three R.F.C. men find themselves drenched by brilliant sunshine. They climb to nine thousand feet, and continue straight ahead, at a hundred miles an hour, deep into enemy territory.

Soon, from a huge bank of fleecy vapor at fifteen thousand, six German scouts—not of the Flying Circus—roar down from the rear. The R.F.C. leader waggles his wings in signals of instruction to Bishop and the other pilot behind him. The boys are trapped unless they use clever strategy. This calls for continuing straight ahead, to lead the Germans to believe that they can make a surprise attack from the rear.

Coming down on an angle and at frightful speed, they are within three hundred yards of their game when the R.F.C. ships, traveling considerably slower, suddenly go upward into inside loops. The Germans find themselves shooting at vanished targets, and they are going too fast to quickly change their course.

As they begin to level off, they find the Britishers coming down *on them*. The last German machine has become separated from the other five, and the R.F.C. leader signals Bishop to take care of that one.

Bishop's first fight!

The ship he's after is a checkered Albatros. Through his mind flash visions of the awful havoc wrought by the "sausages" that have snuffed out defenseless lives in the London night. He thinks, too, of that five-to-one business. And there comes, for a fleeting instant, a picture, sharp and clear, of Margaret Burden of Toronto. One mistake here, and there will be no wedding day with her!

Bishop is suddenly afraid—afraid of gnawing fear itself— as he surges after his quarry. He finds himself within fifty yards of the wings bearing iron crosses. Through the sights he can see black and white checks. He presses that lever on the stick, and he can see the tracer bullets going home.

The Albatros turns over on its back and seems to fall out

of control. Captain Ball has warned Bishop about this. The
Germans have a trick of appearing to be done for, spinning
down from great heights—and then streaking for home. So
Bishop takes nothing for granted. He dives after his prey.
Sure enough, the Albatros begins leveling off two thousand
feet down.

The Canadian goes flashing after it. At not more than
fifty yards, he again sees black and white in his sights. He
presses the lever once more. The Albatros goes into another
spin. Still suspecting a ruse, Bishop, half crazed with fury
now, plummets after it. Down! Down! Down! He is easily
hitting two hundred.

Two thousand feet down, and the German plane is still
falling, careening crazily far to the east and traveling faster
than Bishop, who levels off after the second fusillade. Suddenly it becomes plain to him that the Albatros is doomed.
But he waits—until he sees it hit the ground and burst into
flames.

He is now within fifteen hundred feet of the earth. He
doesn't know that the Nieuport scouts have never been tested
for leveling off from a power dive like this. He does level off,
though, with both wings intact. He breathes hard and smiles.
The figure 1 will go alongside of his name on the blackboard
tonight!

Death reached out for Bishop many times during the next
fortnight, but couldn't quite touch him. The Head Hunters
almost got him a few times—almost. He shot down several
more planes. Ball witnessed some of the scraps, and thoroughly approved. "The chap's either part fool," the British ace
remarked, "or quite the bravest man I've ever seen."

It was on Easter Sunday that Billy Bishop really got
started. Alone and with flying coat over yellow silk pajamas,
he climbed to fifteen thousand feet.

He glances toward the east. One enemy single-seater.
Fair game. He plays dumb and lets the enemy get on his tail.
Then a quick loop, and he's right behind him. Several rounds,
and the German is done for.

There's a balloon over there, a mile away. The ground
crew see Bishop streaking for it. They work frantically to
pull it down. The bag is only three hundred feet from the
earth as the Canadian gets over it. "Onions"—flaming white

missiles—come up as he dives. Throttle wide open, he's coming almost straight down. He presses the Lewis lever at fifty feet. His wheels just miss the top of the crumpling, smoking bag.

An Albatros scout has arrived too late to save the balloon —but now it is right on his tail and he sees it just in time. He'll try something new, something Ball has taught him. He'll make a loop, but will come down *under* the Albatros. Up he loops, just in time to dodge a drumful of lead, and when he completes the circle he's fifty feet below—and there's the black belly of the Albatros in the sights!

The Nieuport quivers as the Lewis rattles. A burst of flame from above—only twenty feet above—from the belly of the Albatros. Bishop's top plane just misses its ground wheels as it goes into a swirling, flaming dive.

Fifteen minutes later he's at ten thousand feet, five miles northeast of Arras. There are two enemy single-seaters far in front of him. After them! Presently he's so close on the tail of one that the other doesn't dare fire. Then the other makes a mistake. He gets out in front and fifty yards beneath. Bishop remembers a diagram of Ball's. He lets the first ship have a drumful, then dives and writes his name on the second one.

He now feels exaltation such as he has never known. He goes stalking, stalking. Ah! Three more checkered birds of prey over toward Vitry! He gets up behind the rear one before they know it. The Lewis speaks with authority again. There were three. Now there are two.

The first ship has not yet hit the ground when Bishop is on the tail of another. He chases this one in crazy circles for three minutes. Then he suddenly notices that the third fellow is nowhere around; has fled to cover. So he writes his name in lead yet again, and swirls alone, triumphant eagle, as he sees a mass of flames careening down.

He has cleared the sky. Six ships and a balloon bagged. The hunt is over for the day.

Ball saw Bishop looking at the blackboard that night. "One of these days," he told him, "your name's going to be first."

"I'll never pass you, captain."

"Yes, you will. I won't be around long. I can't last at the rate I'm going. They're bound to get me soon."

On Easter Monday the Canadians swept over Vimy Ridge. For days after that, youths like Bishop in the air corps were up sometimes as much as eight or ten hours. On the ground, behind the lines, the ever-present specter of Death quickened life. Deep friendships hastily took form. And when the ominous words "Did not return" were scrawled alongside of a name on the blackboard, Bishop's heart would harden. He would hurry out to his plane for target practice. He had obtained a linen target three feet square and placed it in a field. He would go up and dive down on it, firing always to within a hundred feet from the ground. Thus the youth from Ontario sharpened up his firing eye—and this was, in some ways, more dangerous than combat. Sometimes he leveled off so close to the ground that his wheels touched.

Early in May, about six weeks after his first victory, he had the figure 15 alongside of his name, which was right below Captain Ball's. One sunset, when he came in, he saw that his own name now headed the list. *Richthofen's Flying Circus had gotten Captain Ball.*

Bishop's china-blue eyes were misty as he dropped on to a bench under the blackboard and held his head in his hands. He wrote to Miss Burden that night:

They have killed my dear friend—Richthofen and his scarlet gangsters. They are going to pay for this, Margaret!

As the sun was dying one day, Bishop was up with one other machine—the C.O.'s. That morning he had participated in nine engagements in an hour and forty-five minutes, without a decision. The Flying Circus had at last struck below the belt. Several of its members had crossed the British lines, when Squadron Sixty was known to be engaged elsewhere, and dropped maiming missiles.

Over to the north were five specks. Scarlet!

Bishop and the major headed straight for what they knew was going to be a two-to-five hell. They shot up to fifteen thousand feet, then turned, and were presently "sitting" over the enemy.

Margaret Burden's fiancé began a dive. As he got within a thousand feet of the blood-colored machines, the leader left the rest and was presently off by himself. As Bishop went closer, he saw the man in the cockpit waving to him. Closer still, he noticed for the first time something that set that machine apart from the others of the same color. Flying from rudder and wing tips were the streamers of the leader of the circus—the renowned Baron von Richthofen!

PART TWO—DEATH TAKES NO HOLIDAY

THE White Knight of Canada plummets to fifty yards from the Red Knight of Germany. Scarlet shows in the machine-gun sights. Bishop is right on Richthofen's tail. A drumful of lead spatters from the Lewis—but the target has vanished. The wily baron has gone into a lightning loop.

Bishop levels off. He's about to turn his head when something grazes it. Lead from the rear whistles a hole in the windpane up front. The Red Knight has completed his mad circle and zinged down directly behind the Canadian.

At last Billy Bishop has met his match! This enemy, too, is a nonpareil of the heavens. He is to achieve an incredible victory score before Valhalla beckons. Like Bishop, he started in the cavalry, but the mud and slime of static warfare was not his destiny. How singularly, in fact, were the lives of these two to parallel! Richthofen, like Billy Bishop, had been a pupil of his country's master aerial combatant. The brooding Ball had schooled Bishop. The great Boelcke, idol of the Teutons and leader of the dreaded Jagdstaffel II, had taken the nobleman as a fledgling when Richthofen had "escaped" from an uhlan horse regiment. The adept German pupil, like the kid from Owen Sound, Ontario, was to outgrow the multi-league handed-down boots of a departed teacher and to stride on his own winged sandals through the corridors of glory, there to leave his name in fiery letters that would never dim.

Suddenly Bishop is aware of scarlet above, below, and on all sides. The four other Flying Circus boys are chasing the major in his silver Nieuport. Bishop is afraid to fire as he spurts straight up to get out of the melee. Scarlet shows in the sights—but so does silver.

Presently Bishop is upstairs, Richthofen down, and the dogfight is between them. It's obvious that the baron wants the same thing as the Ontario boy—a duel between just the two of them. Bishop sees Richthofen waving, and the four other scarlet ships get out of this private scrap of his.

Bishop goes into a power dive, but the baron wants none of it. He spurts just out of range, like a cool prize-fighter sidestepping a telegraphed roundhouse right. He seems to stand utterly still for an instant, then the scarlet ship twists into position and goes like a meteor after Bishop. As the Canadian, level now, makes a turn to force Richthofen into a difficult broadside shot instead of a tail barrage, the baron fools him. He keeps on going, and presently he's below, surging up right under the silver belly.

Bishop banks to the left, causing the German's lethal pellets to glance, letting the lower right wing take them. Now the two cyclone crazily for well over a minute—Bishop above, Richthofen below. Round one; two coming up.

Now Richthofen uncorks a fast one. He loops high above Bishop and, instead of winding up behind him, comes down on the right side, getting a broadside crack at the Canadian. Bishop, taken off guard, nevertheless manages to start an upward loop himself. He gets off with a tail riddled sidewise.

Bishop comes down, and now it's his turn for a broadside smash at the uhlan. But his gun jams! His heart goes into high and his tongue spouts oaths. But the gun won't work!

Richthofen apparently notices this, for he just dances around as Bishop goes upstairs to try to fix the gun. But he can't get it fixed. Then, first thing he knows, Richthofen and his four comrades are flying away to the east. The battle's off. Whatever dirty tactics members of his squadron have been guilty of, Richthofen personally is chivalry itself. He won't take advantage of a plane with a jammed gun. He grows smaller in the distance. No doubt he entertains thoughts similar to those of Billy Bishop. It is in the cards that these two fabulous fellows will live to meet up there again. . . .

Somehow, the major, who was also a mighty handy individ-

ual with a stick and a Lewis lever, had managed to survive,
and he and the young lieutenant streaked for home.

With death constantly so near, the boys in the Royal Flying
Corps were quick to grasp at straws of humor to relieve the
nightmare that took hold of them after a particularly close
call up there. They were never afraid while actually facing
death. They had to concentrate to such an extent on co-
ordinating mind and muscle that there was no room for
fear. It was only when they hit ground again that they
realized how hideous had been certain minutes in the blue,
and that the same kind of minutes would tick into the present
soon again, perhaps in the next hour.

Bishop had a little poem that he had learned in childhood
that suddenly came to him one day when, in the rarefied
atmosphere four miles up, with a big German machine on his
tail, he found that his tiny scout, because of its minimum
of plane surface, wouldn't take the "bite" that was necessary
for a quick maneuver. As he yanked the stick back as far as
it would go, and bullets from the dealer in death behind him
began to whistle all around, some going through his windpanes, he began to recite aloud:

> "Will you walk a little faster?" said a whiting to a snail;
> "There's a porpoise close behind us, and he's treading
>   on my tail . . ."

Yes, it was pretty close to madness up there at the back
door of heaven. Below, in the deserted French villages that
had been left behind when the Canadians swept over Vimy
Ridge, the daredevils of the skies became playful between
alarms and assignments. If they had the good fortune to
chance upon some unopened supplies in a grogshop, they
would always save a drink or two for the ducks and drakes
of the vicinity. They used to get these flocks drunk by feeding
them bread soaked in brandy. Then they would try to line
them up in flying formation. One day a buddy of Bishop's—a
fellow who never "got the wind up" in the air—rushed into
Sixty Squadron's H.Q., the naturally ruddy color drained
from his face.

"Seen a ghost?" asked Bishop.

"I gave too much drink to a prize drake—and it keeled

over, dead as a doornail," was the reply. "The farmer's enraged. He's going to report me to the C.O. You've got to *do* something, Billy!"

Such was the brand of fear that struck at the R.F.C. aces! Such was the unbalanced sense of proportion of the men who laughed at death, Yes, this was the crazy ink in which the map of Europe was redrawn. And now, a quarter of a century later, when Lieutenant Colonel William Avery Bishop is Marshal of the Royal Canadian Air Force, training youths for combat over the second western front, the same thing is happening again in Europe to kids who were listening to a different kind of rattle back in 1917.

The men of Sixty Squadron had by this time become much attached to the Flying Pig. This man, thus monickered because he was so corpulent that he bulged all over the tiny cockpit of his observation plane, happened to be an enemy. Bishop first spotted him while going over the German lines to skewer a "sausage" one day. The Pig was handling an old box car, and was only a couple of thousand feet up and well behind his own lines. As Bishop flew down to look him over, the Pig, who must have weighed almost three hundred pounds, displayed a singular lack of talent for flying and marksmanship. Greatly excited, he pulled such tactical boners that Bishop decided he wasn't fair game.

Next day, when Bishop was passing over the area with his patrol, there the Pig was again. All six British planes dived after him, sending tracer bullets all around his crate, purposely missing him. Then, as the Pig returned the fire with remarkable inaccuracy, Bishop and the boys pretended to be frightened and "fled."

The Pig no doubt strutted that night, telling all who would listen of his astonishing feat of battling six R.F.C. planes singlehanded.

This went on for several weeks. When a new man came into Sixty Squadron, he would be told about the Flying Pig and admonished not to shoot him down, no matter what the circumstances, because the fat fellow unconsciously afforded so many much-needed laughs. The boys had decided that the Pig had probably been a big shot around Berlin when the war broke out, and despite his lack of native qualifications, had used his influence to become a flyer.

One day a new man came in and reported that he had shot down an observation crate over the German lines. Some one neglected to tell him about the ungainly enemy. Bishop and the others got a description of the doomed craft, which had been set ablaze in midair. "The Pig," they said in grim unison. Glasses were filled and solemnly raised, and a toast was drunk to the man who had, although he didn't know it, come to be Sixty Squadron's most amusing friend.

The infrequent smiles on the faces of the youths were quickly wiped off when, alongside of blackboard names, there appeared with increasing frequency the words "Did not return." The fury that ensued after a dear friend had been killed took various forms. The commanding officer, for example, rushed out after posting a D.N.R. notice one day.

Bishop was apprehensive. In a little while he followed. At the enemy lines, he saw below him a strange sight that he couldn't at first make out. Closer, he noticed a British machine flying upside down only a few hundred feet above the trenches, while the Archies on the ground sent "onions" up at it.

Presently the machine righted itself and started back for home. Bishop recognized the C.O. in the cockpit. His superior told him later that the idea had suddenly dawned on him that the supreme gesture of contempt for the enemy would be to do just what he had done—fly upside down close over their lines while they belched away.

One morning Bishop went far over the enemy front to get a "sausage." On the way, he knocked down in flames an enemy two-seater equipped with a swivel gun. Coming back, flying westward, he saw five enemy craft. Two, observation two-seaters, were lower than the rest. Three scouts were well up and to the rear of the first two.

Calculating quickly, Bishop figured the strong sun in the east would be in the eyes of the enemy, particularly the lower two, as he was in a direct line between them and the sun. He figured to make a surprise running attack on the observation machines before the three others could get down to lend aid. He got a little more than he bargained for this time, though, for as he went headlong at the lower pair and emptied a drum at them, the rear machine maneuvered in such a way that it got on his tail.

He started turning just in time. His rudder was perforated. Again he pulled a trick out of Captain Ball's bag. He came down and stuck so close on the tail of one German that the other was afraid to open up lest he riddle his comrade. Then one of those unexplainable mysteries of the sky came to pass. The other machine flew away. The Canadian caught the remaining machine broadside. He saw the gunner die right in his seat a moment before the ship careened downward, bursting into flames.

Circling around and looking at his handiwork, Bishop forgot momentarily about the three enemy scouts. He glanced up just in time to see them roaring down on him. There was but one thing to do, and he did it. He stuck his nose up at the same angle they were coming at, and they began to straighten out to avoid a collision. As they did, Bishop, with incredible speed, stuck his nose higher still, and found himself pointing directly up at them. He let go, and got the middle one in the belly.

The two remaining craft swirled around to get into position. He was on the tail of one while the other was on his tail. Don't ask me to explain how this man and his plane could have been shot at so many times and not seriously damaged. Maybe Bishop was a favorite of the gods. He was firing at the ship in front of him, and nothing seemed to be happening. He then discovered, as he went up for a loop and leveled off above, that he was out of ammunition.

That was serious. He knew he wasn't fighting Richthofen now, and could expect no mercy, let alone chivalry, from the two who were jockeying around just below him.

He had one possible chance, the outside possibility that this pair had had enough, inasmuch as they had seen him shoot down two planes and chase another since the combat had begun. And so, looking for all the world as if he had ammunition in wholesale quantities, he climbed still higher, looped, seemed for an instant to be frozen in the air, and then began to plunge straight down at the two of them.

As he approached, they separated, giving him a wide berth between them, and he split the ozone at a forty-five-degree angle until he was two thousand feet below them. They had been in the act of getting out of his way as he had plummeted down at them and, he hoped, hadn't noticed that no bullets were coming from his Lewis.

Fortune reached out and grabbed Billy Bishop by the hand. By the time he leveled off below and looked up, there were the two Germans, a thousand feet to the east, streaking for home like winged mammals out of Hades. It was Bishop's first bluff.

Certain of the Head Hunters of Richthofen's Flying Circus were now seeming to concentrate on Allied lame ducks or loners. There was one instance of a fleet of eleven scarlet ships popping from the top side of a cloud and shooting down a single R.F.C. craft. Another time, several enemies pounced on a youngster traveling alone. First, bullets went through his legs. Then his petrol tank was punctured and the escaping vapors ignited the gasoline that had flowed all over the boy. The pursuers couldn't have missed seeing that, but they were not through yet. They actually crossed over the lines, and, before the Britons on the ground could get into the air, the enemy peppered away at the loner's cockpit.

That the plane ever landed was in the nature of a miracle. But it did land and, just as it became totally enveloped in flames, the kid was pulled out by some courageous Tommies. The doctors had no sooner taken one of his legs off than he died. Before he went he said, "I fought as a Tommy in the campaign at Gallipoli. Then I got to where I wanted to be— here in the Flying Corps. I came halfway round the world from Australia to fight the Hun. I don't mind dying, but I hate to go before I even get started."

To his childhood sweetheart and fiancée, lovely Margaret Burden of Toronto, we find Bishop writing:

My Sweetheart:—

I haven't written you for two days. My heart is full these days. We are having the most awful time. Yesterday, Binnie, a friend of mine & 3 others were shot down & today 4 of my flight went under in a scrap. Oh, those damned Huns. I'll pay a few of them off for this, I swear I will. They were such good people and one was at R.M.C. [Royal Military College, Kingston, Ontario] with me. He always flew on my left and then one was such a nice kid, just out & really a very promising pilot.

Yesterday a wire came that I'd been awarded the Military Cross, but it didn't say what for so I don't know whether it is for the collective scrapping of the last 3 weeks or for one particular show. . . . Quite a lot of rot for a little thing. When this reaches you I will be a captain. Oh, swish! . . . I had the greatest letter from you. In a perfect rage about your costume. I should love to see you like . . . Pepita.

And what of Margaret Eaton Burden? He wrote to her almost every day, sometimes several times a day. She has told me that it is doubtful if ever a girl received stranger love letters. Always the boy who had known her since she was five stated exactly what he had been doing between letters: This pal killed. A narrow escape at three-fifteen. Another pal downed in flames. Another close call at four-twenty. Two "Huns" down in flames; "that made my heart feel good, sweetheart, because that's so much less misery they will bring to the world."

News of Bishop's exploits had gotten back to Toronto. Didn't Margaret Burden read the newspapers? Surely she couldn't have been reading of all that fighting that the young man she was going to marry was doing, and still be going on calmly, helping her country at home? But she was. Thoroughbreds don't cry—in public. They go as Pepita to costume balls and look very gay and enchanting. But they read, many times over, paragraphs in letters from the front that say, "And above all, darling, I pray that you do not worry about me." And then they ponder long into the darkness, when the dawn is already over the Devil's Playground overseas and youths are pulling thick flying coats over thin silk pajamas . . .

The brooding Captain Ball's prediction that Bishop, now a captain himself, would surpass him in the number of enemy scalps credited was, in May, 1917, well on the way to fulfillment, and the Canadian boy had been fighting less than two months. Already the figure 20 was alongside his name at the top of the blackboard in H.Q., while Ball had left the number 43 behind him. Bishop was fated, along with Ball and von Richthofen and Boelcke, to join Collishaw and Barker and MacLaren; Fonck, Guynemer, and Nungesser; Rickenbacker, Baracca, Udet, Boss, Linke, and Immelmann, those legendary men with wings who were forever to stalk the halls of glory after Satan took a holiday —for a quarter of a century.

The Germans dropped a note over the British lines, one day, telling just what had happened to Ball. The British ace had had a D.N.R. tag alongside of his name for some time before the note came. Lothar von Richthofen, the Red Knight's younger brother, had received credit for Ball's doom during a general melee deep in Teuton territory. Ball had been buried behind the German lines with full military honors.

Baron von Richthofen himself had now left the front on an extended holiday, suggested by the Kaiser. It would be good propaganda for the hero of the nation to show himself in Berlin. But Richthofen, a shy fellow at heart, had tired of adulation from both males and females, and had retreated to stalk game on the state hunting preserve in Freiburg. Meanwhile, young Lothar, whom even his brother called "the butcher," had been placed in temporary command of the Jagdstaffel II, and he made the most of it. A fellow who always enjoyed a fight to the hilt when the enemy was outnumbered two or three to one, Lothar—or "Stinky," as some Tommies called him—was having the time of his life leading anywhere from ten to twenty of the scarlet ships near great banks of vapor, where they would wait until they spotted an R.F.C. loner or a small patrol. Then Lothar would send one plane down into the clear and thus decoy the R.F.C. boys, whereupon he and his scarlet gang would scoop down upon them and clear the air.

Enraged at this, Captain Bishop, alone, ran the gantlet one day and dropped a note over the German lines. If von Richthofen wanted a fight, let him kindly communicate with Captain Bishop, Sixty Squadron, R.F.C. Captain Bishop would be pleased to oblige at any place specified, either between the lines or in German territory. The only stipulation was that von Richthofen should be accompanied by not more than two other planes and that these planes would not join in the combat unless von Richthofen were downed.

Bishop waited anxiously for an answer. The Germans were forever dropping notes, usually to inquire as to what had become of a missing comrade, so that they could let his folks know the details. There was really considerable Alphonse-and-Gaston byplay of this sort between the opposed flyers, and all communications were promptly and courteously answered. But no answer came to Billy Bishop from Lothar von Richthofen, and so the Canadian dropped another note just after he had spitted a couple of observation "sausages." This note asked Lothar von Richthofen what the trouble was. So that "Stinky" would have no trouble in identifying Bishop, he was advised that the nose of the Canadian's ship was painted a light blue; the only British ship so marked. Lothar was informed that Bishop was leaving shortly for a vacation in England and wished Lothar, in the meantime, would be courteous enough to accept his challenge.

But Lothar was having none of Bishop—none on the specified terms, anyway. Lothar had never been in a man-to-man scrap in his life, and he didn't intend to start with the Canadian. Bishop's plane had by this time become known behind the enemy lines. The blue-nose business had come about in this manner:

The Germans had gone gaudy. For want of anything better to do, they had painted their scouts green with yellow noses; red bodies with green wings; light blue bodies with red wings; silver bodies, gold noses; khaki bodies with gray planes; and, of course, black and white checks all over.

The boys on the British side had been rather taken with this, but their movement to outhue the enemy was an abortive one, H.Q. supplying the cold water. Bishop got the farthest. His admiring ground crew had, without his knowledge, got hold of some paint the exact color of his eyes and had applied it to the nose of his silver Nieuport.

So now Bishop, as Baron von Richthofen had once been, was a very distinguishable target. Some of the R.F.C. flying men who had landed in enemy territory to be taken prisoners, but who had been accorded the privilege of writing to their comrades across the lines, had told Bishop that the Germans were now discussing the Blue Nose.

Angered at what he was convinced was cowardice on the part of the Red Knight's younger brother, the White Knight, with furlough papers in his pocket, went fighting mad. Goaded by fury, he stalked the skies alone, often deep in enemy terrain. He knocked down balloons, scouts, and ships that were directing artillery fire. He busted up many a "Hun" V formation, singlehanded, by pulling Ball's trick of sticking close on a particular tail. He liked nothing better than to catch a loner before breakfast. His official corroborated record didn't tell the half of it. A German prisoner told of disgust among German artillerymen who had seen three of their own ships darting home to mama when there was nothing visible except a single silver plane with a blue nose— but coming like hell!

Bishop continued to lead a charmed life in a strange land where Death never took a holiday. He was the wonder of all his associates. Almost every day now he was spending eight or more hours in the air. And—talk about the postman on his day off! At the end of a day of a score of combats, with perhaps two or more planes brought down, Bishop would fly off toward the setting sun to relax! When he wasn't making ducks and drakes drunk, he was sharpening up his shooting eye by diving at that ground target that he always kept near H.Q.

His holiday in England was uneventful on the surface. Whereas Richthofen had lunched with the Kaiser and been received by Hindenburg and Ludendorff, Bishop went to the movies, and visited the relatives of dear friends who had been killed. He was going to stay away only a fortnight. Like a duck out of water, he was jumpy at first. The German Head Hunters had only made him blazing mad; London traffic actually frightened him.

The metropolis seemed strange and tame. Hunters shouldn't stay in cities; they should get back to the woods and stalk. This particular hunter belonged high in the blue. Time was being wasted. His was a charmed life. The Grim Reaper had beckoned to him dozens of times, and he had ignored the Reaper's crooked finger. He should be back at the front telling new green kids how to ignore it. The longer he stayed here, the more lives would be lost in Squadron Sixty.

He returned unexpectedly. There was a joyous reunion with the boys of Sixty Squadron—a reunion that was marred, however, by the absence of several familiar faces and voices.

The old fury came over Bishop, and he began to cast about in his mind for a satisfying way to vent it.

His first flights after his return caused him to realize that something had happened to him. He found himself shying away from the one-to-three engagements that had once been his meat. His marksmanship was off. Ships he would normally have bagged with his eyes closed were now getting away.

He was no longer dead certain of himself; with his fleet Nieuport, his slightest whim was no longer a command. London had given fear a chance to get in its hideous handiwork. He had unconsciously regained his perspective in England, and now he realized, as he took to wings again, just how dreadful this business of aerial combat really was.

The Germans had spotted the return of the Blue Nose. Almost daily Bishop's ground crew had to replace windpanes in front of the cockpit. Bullets dancing off his motor and the instrument board being splintered were becoming familiar sights and experiences to him, the Nonpareil.

He had once slept like a child while the big guns talked. Now he told Margaret Burden in his daily letters that he was hardly sleeping at all.

He knew he was useless now unless he licked the enemy behind his own lines, the enemy right in H.Q.—right, in fact, inside himself. It took time. He started the old target practice, diving at the crate on the ground. He gathered all the tin cans and cardboard boxes he could lay hands on, went up, tossed them out and dived, gunning at them.

He didn't give himself a minute to think of himself. He'd putter around his plane, take on any odd job around the airdrome, until he was so physically exhausted that sleep came to him once again. Strangely enough, over the lines, the Red Knight was undergoing virtually the same experience after his lay-off. Richthofen, in fact, would not now go out alone. Never would he travel without at least two "bodyguards" to stand by in the sky in case he needed help.

Gradually, like blood beginning to flow once more through a paralyzed limb, the old mastery, the old cunning, the old to-hell-with-'em spirit came back to Billy Bishop. He had earned it, so he set out again for his hunting grounds in the uncharted heavens.

One day he suddenly found himself trapped by six Head

Hunters who had been lurking in a huge cloud formation. He surged straight up under them, got two, disorganized the other four, and streaked for home, laughing hysterically.

If there was one thing that made Bishop more furious than anything else, it was these Head Hunters. He sat around H.Q. that night, smoking and thinking, ignoring a good time in the next room where a tin-pan piano was all but drowned out by off-key baritones. Next day was his day off. He had been in the habit of spending that wandering, in loud pajamas and bedroom slippers, through a nearby spring-kissed orchard. But he wasn't taking tomorrow off. He summoned an orderly and left a call for three A.M.

Just before dawn, Captain Bishop was streaking into the east at a hundred and twenty miles an hour. At last he found what he was searching for, something on which to drive the final nail in the coffin of Fear. There was an enemy airdrome below. From a mile up, Bishop counted seven planes outside their hangars. As he dropped down in a narrowing spiral, he saw the ground crews were already out, and that the propellers of four of the seven ships were whirring.

He was deep in enemy terrain; and nobody back at Squadron Sixty had any idea where he was, for he had confided in no one as to how he proposed to spend his day off. That flashed through his mind, and so did tender thoughts of Margaret Burden. He always thought of her when he found himself in a spot like this.

Miss Burden must have tossed fitfully in her slumber, if indeed she was asleep at all, at that moment when Billy Bishop, trying to shake off *an awful dread that had suddenly banged back,* drew a deep breath, bit his lower lip, and, with his finger on the machine-gun lever, began to streak like a silver meteor down, down, down on the busy airdrome.

PART THREE—THE RED KNIGHT

TURNS YELLOW

THE White Knight certainly caught that airdrome with its wings down. He was within five hundred feet of it, roaring earthward at forty-five degrees, before the mechanics around four of the seven ships saw what was coming and made for the hangars. At three hundred feet, Bishop pressed the Lewis' trigger and began to rake the runways. Several men dropped, and the Blue Nose made a lightning hairpin turn at the east end of the drome and swept over it once more, within a hundred feet of the ground.

As he returned again, sweeping from west to east, Bishop saw one of the planes taxiing across the field. It was pointed west, ideal for what he had in mind. It was barely off the ground when he flew down to within fifty feet of the runway, pouring everything he had into the tail of his quarry. He couldn't miss. The machine fell into a sideslip and plunged to the ground, a mass of wreckage.

Bishop took what might have been his hundredth chance on tearing off a wing by making another hairpin turn. As he rushed back, a second machine was just bouncing into the air at the end of the field farthest from him. Split seconds were vital now, for there were still two more ships down there that might take off any moment, and he had to attend to this fellow before that happened. He let go again from a hundred yards. The German sailed into a tree and instantly caught fire.

Two down and two to go! Bishop figured the three silent planes wouldn't get into the fray because they couldn't be warmed up fast enough. He turned and saw the two remaining warmed-up ships taking the air *at right angles to each other*. He raked the airdrome again while thinking things over. He decided that perhaps it was best that the planes had separated. He couldn't go after both of them at once, but neither could both of them come after him.

He jumped through the air, as if he were on an undulating slide, as he shot past the hangars this time. For the ground gunners had swung into action now and the air was alive with whining lead. Fortune again smiled on Billy Bishop—or, rather, continued to smile. The machine-gun fire raked the Blue Nose from propeller to rudder but somehow missed the pilot.

As one of the two machines that were now in the air flew straight ahead, the other was going far to the south. The motor of the one nearer to Bishop was apparently still cold, and the plane wasn't making very good time. Bishop's motor, on the other hand, was by this time as hot as he was.

He climbed a thousand feet after his quarry, which meanwhile circled back to a point almost directly over the drome. The other machine was coming for the same spot, too. Not bad strategy on the part of the two German flyers. It was obvious that they had talked this over hastily before going up, the idea being to lead him into a trap over the gunners, with one ship ahead of him while the other sneaked up from behind.

But Bishop was having none of that. He stopped pursuing the one he had gone up after and made a beeline for the other one. This flyer got scared and turned. Now Bishop swung around, and found that the first fellow had tried to sneak up from the rear.

It was all over now—all but a drumful and another crash. Bishop spattered his initials on the third ship and dealt it out of the war. He was about to streak after the fourth one, now quite some distance away, when he noticed five planes high overhead. Had the airdrome telephoned for help? On the theory that it had, the Ontario boy decided to call it a morning and go back for breakfast. He hopped, skipped, and jumped over the airdrome twice more, using every shot of the ammunition he had left on the ground gunners and the three remaining planes, then streaked to the west.

He soon found that he was in the clear. but he hadn't eaten, and a dizziness came over him. He shook his head frantically to clear it, but no dice. Then that old fear climbed into the cockpit with him. He thought of Margaret Burden, his fiancée in Toronto, of the charm of the London drawing rooms where he had been so recently, and then of that churned and blood-caked ground below him and what he had just gone through.

"I guess I actually lost consciousness for a moment or two," he told me recently. "But I somehow got back. In my search for an airdrome to take, I had lost my way. I didn't know until later that I had transacted all that business nearly twenty miles from our own lines."

Bishop dropped some flares when he got home. That meant he had come in with a success story. The ground crew swarmed around the Blue Nose, wondering where the pilot had been so early on his day off.

Modestly, he made his story brief. As he was talking he noticed the ground crew circling around him, eyeing him from head to foot.

"What the devil are you looking at—or for?" he asked.

"We were just wondering, captain," said one fellow, "how it's possible you weren't hit. Have you looked at your machine at all, sir?"

It was only then Bishop realized how much fire he had gone through. The Nieuport looked like a sieve.

Some one, speaking more prophetically than he realized, said, "You'll get the Victoria Cross for this."

That didn't seem to mean a thing to the youth from Owen Sound. "I should be kicked instead," he said. "I botched it. It wasn't the way I planned it at all. I came away with three. *I should have got the fourth!*"

German prisoners captured soon afterward confirmed all that he had written in his official report about his attack on the airdrome.

It was a singular letter that Bishop wrote to his fiancée on June 6, 1917, the day following his call on the airdrome. Here are excerpts:

My Sweetheart,

I didn't write you yesterday. I had a very busy day. I rose at 3 a.m. and flew over to a Hun airdrome, where I did very cunning battle in the way of shooting many wee folks. I opened fire at 7 machines

on the ground. . . . One machine then took off and
I went down to 50 ft. for him & got him. Another
one doing the same crashed into some trees. Then 2
came off together. I climbed to 1000 ft. and did
battle with one & crashed him 300 ft. from the airdrome. I tried to get away.

Monday

I had to stop above and go up after a Hun who
was playing about. To go on with the above story.
I tried . . .

Certainly not an elaborate letter, considering what it was
about. But that was Billy Bishop. Always conservative—
except when in the air.

Unfortunately, there were but a handful of R.F.C. boys
who were meeting with a degree of success that could be
mentioned in the same breath with his exploits. The casualties were appalling. One day Squadron Sixty lost eleven ships
and pilots in twelve hours. There was a bad stretch of sixteen days during which twenty-three boys were brought
down, many of them by the Head Hunters of Richthofen's
Flying Circus. One member of the Circus at this time was a
young man who was deep in dastardly work that was to
equip him for cold-blooded deeds in later years. His name
was Hermann Goering.

New flyers and new planes were coming up from the
bottom of a seemingly fathomless supply pit. Some of the
kids were sent up with Captain Bishop when they'd had but
a score of hours in the air. The truth of the matter was
that new German machines were a little too good for the
Nieuport scouts. Then, too, the Germans were resorting
more and more to tactics that turned the stomachs of the
Englishmen.

Most of the R.F.C. casualties were striplings who didn't
know the ropes—or the German trick of hiding behind or
on top of cloud banks. The fate of the lame ducks and the
loners had usually been witnessed by other R.F.C. craft too
far away to do anything. When a patrol of six British machines went down together, more often than not it was suspected, and later established, they had run into the "road
company" of the Flying Circus, usually headed by Baron

von Richthofen's brother Lothar. There was also a new German squadron, with more than a score of brilliant green planes, that delighted in making mincemeat out of loners.

Bishop studied the H.Q. blackboard one day shortly after the airdrome episode. He suddenly realized that not a single name that had been up there when he had come into the squadron was still there. All new, innocent kids.

New planes were being sent on so fast that there was little or no opportunity to test them. Sometimes a wing would break off and the pilot would be killed before he had so much as set eyes on enemy terrain.

Bishop took a patrol of five green boys out one afternoon. He was still only twenty-three himself, mind you. The instructions were to go over the lines and shoot down anything in sight. Bishop landed back two hours later with just about enough wing surface left to bite the air. He'd been through another of those afternoons that give him nightmares even today, a quarter of a century later.

"On this particular occasion," the White Knight told me, "finding myself with pilots not sufficiently familiar with their new machines or with the country, I instructed them to fly around the airdrome and become familiar with both, but on no account to approach the lines.

"I said I would do the patrol myself, because I knew it would be much safer for me alone than with a complete patrol of inexperienced pilots, which would be no help but instead a liability, as in case of trouble I would have had to protect them myself."

The major in command of the squadron decided to take some pictures of enemy terrain. A crack photographer, he was going to take these himself. One of the regular lens lads had gone ten miles into German territory, with an elaborate escort, and then had snapped the wrong stuff! So the major, in lofty dudgeon, was going to see that no error was made this time.

He made an "appointment" with Bishop's patrol. Its six scouts were to meet him in the air at six thousand feet just east of Arras at nine thirty in the morning. Captain Bishop got to the spot just two minutes early, and the six planes circled around waiting for the major, a punctual, exacting gentleman. A plane was spotted off to the west. Bishop shot out a red flare and the plane answered in kind. It was the major, all right.

The idea was that the patrol was to fly a couple of thousand feet above the major while he went within a thousand feet of the ground for his photographs. He had a skillful pilot, but his plane was a job that hadn't been put together for combat.

Deep in enemy terrain the major suddenly began his descent. The patrol was to follow. But just then Bishop spotted four enemy scouts in the distance. There was a handy cloud, and he led the way into it. Thus the enemy could see the major but not the six scouts of the patrol.

Bishop kept his eye on the second hand of his watch until he figured the four Germans would be nearing what they thought was a loner. Then he popped out of the cloud. Sure enough, they were swooping down upon the major, and now Bishop and his five pals swooped on *them*.

The major, meanwhile, saw the four enemy planes coming at him and angrily wondered what under heaven had happened to his interference.

Presently the Germans were as surprised as he had been. The Blue Nose shot one down in flames, and another of the patrol accounted for a second before its pilot knew what struck him. The two remaining Germans fled.

The major got his pictures and everybody started back. Bishop was expecting a severe reprimand, if not punishment, for using his superior officer as a decoy. He was quick and lavish with apologies and explanations when the party landed.

The major listened sternly. Then he broke into a smile. "Carry on," he said to Bishop. "I don't mind being used for a decoy any time you can shoot down a couple of those ——s. The only thing that worried me when I thought they surely had me was the fact that I was carrying quite a bit of money on my person. I should have hated those pigs to have taken that from my body!"

Well along in June it became obvious to Bishop and to other members of Sixty Squadron that there was a concerted effort on the part of the enemy to get his troublesome Blue Nose. Many times, when he was flying over the German lines in a patrol, their Archies sent up explosive tokens that looked to be intended exclusively for him. Just to make certain, the boys would sometimes separate when they were right over the lines. Sure enough, the Blue Nose was the one ship the enemy gunners would pick out.

This didn't scare Bishop but it made him sore. Or, to use his own words, "I was annoyed—frankly." So he retaliated. When he couldn't find any "game" in the sky, he'd fly to within a hundred feet of the German trenches and open up. By this time the Blue Nose had been hit so often and patched up so much, and had had so many parts replaced, that very little of the original machine was left.

"But I liked that little ship," the Marshal says today, "because it had brought me through so many tight squeezes. I didn't want to part with it for another, although new and faster ships were on the way for us."

It was at this time that Richthofen's Flying Circus was really going to town. The baron, after his lengthy "vacation," had never seemed to regain his old cunning as Bishop had. Richthofen was now very much like a temperamental but fading star baseball pitcher who picks his spots. He was never seen in the skies alone, and seldom beyond his own lines. Always he was accompanied by from two to thirty "bodyguards." The Circus was concentrating more than ever on lame ducks and cumbersome observation machines that didn't stand a chance once their patrol of six was pounced upon by twenty or more scarlet ships.

Bishop, on the other hand, was constantly over the enemy lines. His score was mounting. He had now passed the figure 30 on the H.Q. blackboard. Often he was up alone, on flights that were called unauthorized because he made them on his days off, with destination unannounced. He was now growing somewhat more cautious when leading a patrol, but only out of consideration for the other fellows. His confidence in himself had bounded back full blast, and his shooting was near deadly perfection.

Sometimes it wasn't easy to find any German planes in the area assigned to Sixty Squadron. In such a case he would shop around and find out where there was something doing. When he got hold of such information, he called it "a good tip." Then, out of his own territory altogether, he would spend his day off helping flyers in other squadrons.

He got in a bad jam one day, and saw a sample of

courage that he has never ceased to admire. Six Head Hunters came down on him. By quick maneuvering he managed to get to his favorite spot—above them. He had played dumb when they had come down, then looped up fast.

Now he sat upstairs, looking them over. They went into a formation in layers of two. He dived on the top layer, and although he didn't bring anybody down, he apparently did some damage, for one of the ships flew away.

Up he went again. By this time the other top-layer ship had gone off to one side and below. Bishop took another dive at the two now on top, sprayed them, and went up again.

The fight was taking place close to a great cloud bank. Suddenly out of the white vapor came a silver ship of the R.F.C. It was five against one, the pilot of the new arrival saw at a glance. So he streaked toward Bishop to join the scrap.

What happened then Bishop couldn't, at the moment, understand. As this other plane came forward, the five Germans fled. The new arrival showed a decided disinclination to follow them—which wasn't in keeping with his behavior just previously. He waved to Bishop and the two made for home.

"Sorry I couldn't be of more help," said the other man, back at the airdrome. "You see, I was flat out of ammunition."

"And you knew that when you came over to help me?" asked Bishop.

"Sure thing. But I took a chance. *They* didn't know I was out, so I figured, inasmuch as I had come from a cloud, they'd think perhaps there were more of the R.F.C. behind me, and go away. Which they apparently thought, and certainly did."

"But if your bluff hadn't worked you'd have been in a fine spot," said Bishop. "They'd have got you sure."

The other flyer—a New Zealander—laughed. "Well, you were in a spot, too. As well two as one, you know."

It wasn't long after Bishop's single-handed attack on the airdrome that he had his second meeting with Richthofen. He and his patrol were ambuscaded by Head Hunters one day and a dogfight began about seven thousand feet up—Bishop's favorite height for battle, not too high and not so low that the Archies could bother him.

It took Bishop quite a few minutes to spot Richthofen himself. In a dogfight the Canadian always went upstairs as quickly as possible and sat there until he saw a chance to come down to advantage. It was while he was sitting upstairs that Richthofen apparently saw him. The Red Knight got off to one side. The second combat between the two knights was about to begin.

They recognized each other at the same moment. The Canadian circled a few times while the German danced around. Then Bishop feinted as if going into a loop, but instead twisted the Blue Nose into diving position and came down on Richthofen's tail. The baron side-stepped and seemed to be about to go into a loop himself, and then to come down on Bishop's tail.

But Bishop fooled him. The Owen Sound boy had perfected in-and-out fighting by this time. He was adept at leveling off and going up again, instead of plunging straight down. This entailed no end of strain on the wings, but the Blue Nose had never failed him yet.

Bishop came down on Richthofen a second time, got close to the Uhlan's rudder, and spilled a drum at the scarlet ship. Instantly the Red Knight fell into a spin—a hideous swirling spin. It looked like certain doom. Bishop was so surprised that he just sat there watching the baron go down, down, down, while the melee went on at one side of him.

Ordinarily he would have suspected a ruse and have dived right after the falling plane. But he didn't suspect the Red Knight of one. No; Richthofen would have stayed up there and dueled to the death. This could mean but one thing— Richthofen was in a death spin.

Down and down went the scarlet ship—a thousand feet, two thousand, three thousand, four, until it seemed to be nearing the ground. Bishop looked up for an instant, to see what was happening in the melee. When he looked down again, the Richthofen plane had righted itself! *It wasn't coming back, either.* It was streaking like a bat out of hell for the east—and home. It was too late to catch it.

Billy Bishop was the most disappointed man in Europe. Heavens, if the Red Knight wouldn't fight him alone, who would? That vacation in Germany, when Richthofen had received the plaudits of the multitude, apparently had done the nobleman no good.

The R.F.C. boys got out of the scrap with whole skins if not whole planes. The mix-up wound up as a Mexican stand-off. Bishop's admiration for Richthofen was definitely liquidated.

By this time the R.F.C. was beginning to have less and less respect for the renowned Flying Circus. Even German prisoners were admitting that it was an open secret behind the "Hun" lines that the baron, once the personification of courage and gallantry, was now running up his score by picking his spots. Other members of the Circus had to move aside when there was an easy and sure kill, so that the nobleman could get the credit for it.

Bishop and some of the other boys in Sixty Squadron got a bulging sow from a neighboring barnyard, painted it scarlet and put the letters R-i-c-h-t-h-o-f-e-n across its back, tied it with ribbons, and took it back to the barnyard. The other swine regarded "Richthofen" with such bewilderment that they wouldn't associate with it for days, until the paint began to wear off!

Strange things were happening in the skies. Hermann Goering and nineteen of his pals were out looking for loners one day when a silver craft popped from a cloud bank. It flew straight ahead—right at the oncoming Head Hunters. Two of them opened fire point-blank, then swung aside to avoid a collision.

Right through the formation, straight as an arrow, went the R.F.C. ship, its pilot looking directly in front of him, turning neither to right nor left. Goering and another German climbed up, then came down on the tail of the strangely acting craft. They gave it everything they had. Still it kept on its straight, level course. Others dived at it, riddling it from nose to rudder, but it kept right on going.

For five minutes the Germans swarmed about the silver thing, firing, firing, firing. It made no move to duck nor to return the fire. They had never seen anything like it. Finally Goering flew close alongside of the plane. Then he gave a signal, and the Head Hunters turned and went in the opposite direction, while the silver ship went on out of sight.

The explanation was that its pilot had gone west long before, but at the moment his controls had been in neutral and the throttle wide open, and so the derelict of the skies had sailed on and on with a corpse in the cockpit.

It wasn't all cakes and ale for Captain Bishop. In the beginning of July the cards started turning against him. He was up alone, late one afternoon, when he spotted a German two-seater in the distance, making for the British lines. He started after it, but it climbed out of sight.

Scouting about, Bishop got a glimpse of his game again. Again the German started to climb, and so did he. At 19,500 feet both ships leveled off, and Bishop started for the enemy head on. He fired, but his target swerved. As it passed within ten feet, the gunner in the rear opened up with pom-pom balls. If one of those pretty little white puffs came too close to a pilot's face, he wouldn't have a face any more.

A lot of the balls burst around the Blue Nose, but Bishop wasn't hit. He made a hairpin turn and saw that the German was now above him. He hadn't noticed until now that his right hand and part of his arm were utterly lifeless because of the intense cold more than three miles up. He had been so intent on the chase that he hadn't thought of himself.

With a great effort, he jerked the stick to point the nose up so that he could get a crack at the enemy's belly. Jerking the nose up like that caused him to lose speed; the air was too thin for the planes to bite; and the next thing Bishop knew, he was in a hideous swirling dive, completely out of control.

Down he went, half conscious. He doesn't know to this day just what happened. He tells me he must have acted instinctively. Two miles below his head suddenly cleared and he found himself coming out of the dive with his left hand tugging at the stick, his right arm at his side, limp.

His number wasn't up yet—but he was through for that day.

The arm, of course, came around all right. Bishop was open for lethal business next day as usual. By this time the boys, in their rare moments of relaxation, were enjoying all the comforts of home. They had had their tennis rackets and white flannels shipped on to them, and had begun a tournament on an improvised court.

One day Bishop won a match. He decided to celebrate by going up and bagging a "Hun." It was his day off, so he went alone. His score was nearing 40 now, and he wanted to run it up before his next leave, the following month. There was an outside chance that he might get sufficient time off to get married on that next leave.

Near the enemy lines he saw three German scouts. Ordinarily he would have climbed high above them, his favorite method in one-to-three business. But he admits that this day he was a little careless because, as he puts it, "Familiarity bred contempt." And so, instead of climbing, he went toward the three, which were traveling in a V in the same direction as he was. He thought he'd spring a little surprise from below.

He got to within a hundred yards of the rear of them and was only a hundred feet below when he himself got the surprise of his life. They had been playing possum. They had, in fact, undoubtedly planned this well, for they bore the markings of a squadron that had come to no end of grief at the hands of the stalking, quarrelsome Blue Nose.

Before Bishop realized it, all three ships made hairpin turns and started down at him. They had gravity with them, and therefore speed. He, on the other hand, was climbing at the moment, and traveling at snail's pace in comparison. Closer and closer they came, now nicely abreast. Whether Bishop went up, down, or sideways, they would draw first blood—the important blood. And now, as he involuntarily ducked his head, the guns of all three, as if operating on a single level, belched crimson.

PART FOUR—THE GOERING GANG

THE bullets from the three German planes whined through the Blue Nose and the rear of the cockpit was riddled. The fact that Bishop had ducked his head when he did saved his life. Then, too, something like a miracle had happened. While the Blue Nose was riddled, it had apparently been struck in no vital spot, for the motor was still functioning perfectly. The Germans had been so overjoyed at this chance to down the Canadian that their marksmanship had suffered!

Bishop looked over his shoulder. The three "Huns" were going into turns again, and they were above him, giving them continued advantage. There was no question about it; they had Bishop now. They had muffed one chance; it was hardly likely they would miss a second time.

Bishop's mind worked faster than it is possible to relate. From a flashing stream of consciousness came vital thoughts. The Germans knew who he was, from that blue nose on his silver ship. They knew his reputation for causing trouble, battling against overwhelming odds, and they would expect him to fight.

He could make just one move: borrow a trick from their bag and go into a spin—something he had never before deliberately done.

He had been so intent on creeping up under the trio that he had not looked at what was below him. He glanced down now, and saw something made to order for him. A huge bank of clouds directly below and not a thousand feet away.

The Germans were on the way back after him now. He laughed. His luck was still holding. He kicked the rudder and went into a swirling nose dive, apparently out of control. Straight down he went, and presently everything around him was blotted out. He was right in the cloud bank. He couldn't pull himself out of the spin there. There was no way of knowing how far down the vapor extended. It might go so close to the ground that leveling off would be out of the question when he got below the ceiling.

Well, you only die once. Better to die voluntarily crashing than have the enemy send you down in flames. And he'd had his fun. The hunting had been great while the season was open. Too bad, though, that he had to go now, when he was still below Ball's record of 43. His hero, dark and brooding, would be looking down from Valhalla and would be disappointed.

But the departed Captain Ball must have grinned grimly. For Billy Bishop, his star pupil, popped through the ceiling with more than three thousand feet to spare! Fortune, and his wings, stood by him once again. He somehow leveled off. The three Germans were nowhere in sight. They had apparently taken it for granted that they had got him when they saw the Blue Nose go into that spin.

Bishop laughed all the way home. But when he got back he had words of advice for all to hear:

"Don't ever get careless. I just did, out there—and I'm a lucky fool to be back telling about it."

Superiority in the air had seesawed back and forth between the Allies and the Germans. First England had it. Then Germany. Then England again. And now the Germans, with their improved Albatroses and Gothas, had the edge once more.

But in July, 1917, the Royal Flying Corps got a shipment of the new S. E. 5s. There were two machine guns which operated from a single lever on these, instead of just the one that the Nieuports had. The boys in Sixty Squadron soon learned, too, that the manufacturer's claim that these ships would do twenty-five miles an hour more than the Nieuports wasn't an exaggeration. Measured miles behind the lines established that.

Bishop began to worry. Rumors about him started circulating among the flyers. They'd be in little knots, whispering, when he'd bounce into H.Q. and suddenly the talk would cease. He couldn't find out what it was all about.

Then a friend told him: "You'll be going back to be

decorated. And there's a lot of talk about you not coming back here."

"What!" This was the worst news Billy Bishop could have heard—this ominous word that they were going to take him out of the air. He knew the implication all too well. An executive post, probably as a major. A lot of high-sounding words from the War Office about his being an inspiration to fledgling flyers, and how he was too valuable a man to risk in the air. A lot of medals and braid and formality. No more pulling your coat over loud pajamas and going up for a "Hun" or two before breakfast. No more hunting up there in the gray and the blue. No more close calls that gave you a bang no hunter had ever known, except these others who stalked the biggest of all game.

Yes, Billy Bishop was in the strange position of losing the job he loved best for the simple reason that he was too good at it. Well, there was one consolation. Maybe it would take some time for the official routine to grind him out of the front and into Buckingham Palace for an investiture by the King, and there was always his day off. He could do as he pleased then. After all, this was his own life.

He won't admit it today, but those who knew him at the time will tell you that when he got that fast ship, he used to slip away on his day off, and come in late for morning mess with an enemy scalp or two to his credit—and afraid to report the scraps for fear they'd clamp down on him tighter than ever. The C.O. wasn't sending him up so much now, except when there was a particularly important job to do; and that, to the boy from Owen Sound, Ontario, was the handwriting on the wall.

He had his new S.E. painted red, white, and blue. The Germans were quick to spot it, aided no doubt by the fact that Bishop himself angrily dropped a note over their lines, one day, advising them of a change in ships and describing his new one! It was the same old story. Try as he did to pick a man-to-man fight, nobody would fight him.

After all, the German airmen weren't to be blamed in a way. Would *you* fight Joe Louis?

The enemy were laying elaborate traps for the White Knight toward the end of July. The result was, he got himself into an eighteen-carat jam one morning before breakfast. That was one of his favorite times to go out after the braver of the early birds; and by this time he had brought down so many observation machines that he had lost count. One fine morning, when the clouds were big and thick and he was sailing along looking for game, he saw, under a cloud bank, a big juicy two-seater.

Brave but not foolish, Bishop suspected a trap, particularly when, as he spurted after the German, the ship gave no evidence of wanting to mix it, but sped on to the far or east side of the cloud and well below the bottom of the bank. Bishop knew right then that some Head Hunters were playing around on that side of it and had sent the loner to decoy him in their direction.

Just for the hell of it, he decided to take a peek. His strategy was all planned. When he saw the boys out in the clear on the far side, he would turn and go up into the cloud, flying westward, before they would have a chance to come down on him.

Well, they were there all right—Hermann Goering and some of his pals. So Bishop made a hairpin turn and shot up into the bank, heading away from them. He came out on the topside of it, well above and to the west of the Goering gang —only to meet with one of the major surprises of his flying days. The Germans had anticipated his maneuver, and others of the Flying Circus boys, whom he hadn't been able to see until now, had been lurking *above* the cloud. And now they were ready to chop him up into little pieces.

But, instead, it was their turn for a surprise. He dived right back into the white fluff and came out of the bottom, on the homeward side. His quick reaction had so taken the enemy aback that they had apparently just stayed up there, too stunned to do anything.

Eventually, when they saw him streaking for home, they went after him. Here's where the fleetness of the new S.E. came in. He left them far behind and got back from one of the Germans' most elaborate traps for him without so much as a single bullet hole in his ship.

The Flying Fish appeared about this time. Bishop never did find out who this fellow was. He operated in conjunction with several enemy squadrons, usually playing a decoy role. He was called the Fish because, one day when Bishop got a good look at him, he saw that his ship had a finish of silver scales. This was by all odds the most unusual paint job ever done behind the German lines, and it wrought no end of confusion among the R.F.C. boys, because the Fish at a distance looked like one of their comrades.

One day Captain Bishop thought he had caught the Fish with his fins down. The Canadian had been all around a nearby cloud bank and had seen no sign of any other ships. When he went after the scaled fellow, several enemy ships bobbed out of nowhere. Bishop still doesn't know where they came from. Certainly a formation wouldn't have gone inside a cloud where the chances of crashing would have been manifold.

This time the enemy formed a fire-belching wall between Bishop and his own lines. Bad business, that. There was but one thing he could do—surprise them. They would expect him to try to get through, and there they were, every one of them above him. A sixty-mile gale was blowing against him. He figured he could show them some speed with this new crate of his if he were traveling with instead of against that gale.

So he turned and sped toward Germany! The gale and the S.E. fell in love, and Bishop has never traveled faster in his life. He put more and more distance between himself and the pursuing slower Albatroses. Eventually he lost them altogether. But by this time he was thirty miles inside the German lines, and dusk was coming on. The gale would work against him on the way back.

He climbed up to more than three miles, fearing that he would run into other German squadrons. But gradually a soothing darkness enveloped him, and he flew by his instruments. It took him more than an hour to get back, and when he did he dropped flares and they had to flood the airdrome for him to land.

It was in August that Captain Bishop received the bad news. He was instructed to leave the front and proceed to London, where further instructions would be given him. There were sad farewells. Something told him he wouldn't be back. Up on the H.Q. blackboard, alongside of the name W. A. Bishop, there was the astounding figure 47. That represented four more planes than had been sent swirling, crashing to destruction by the brooding Captain Ball.

The slim blond young man from Ontario was becoming a living legend. He called back over his shoulder, as he walked out to the car that was to take him on the first leg of his journey to London, "I'll be back. They can't do this to me!"

And—this prospect presaged his worst scare of the entire wartime—he was going to Buckingham Palace to stand before King George to receive three medals at once: the Victoria Cross, highest decoration for valor within the gift of the monarch; the Distinguished Service Order; and the Military Cross. The Victoria Cross was for that little early-morning affair when he had riddled the German airdrome.

Much against his hidden inclinations, Bishop attended a dinner in his honor the night he arrived in London. A big dance followed. The modest twenty-three-year-old from Owen Sound was desperately unhappy, and he said so in a letter written after the dance to his fiancée, Margaret Burden of Toronto. "I should be in the air, Margaret," he wrote, "not on the ground. I'm afraid they're going to make me a major. A friend told me."

PART 5—CONCLUSION

BISHOP arrived at Buckingham Palace next morning at ten ten. The investiture was to be at ten thirty. He was trembling. Any fears he had known in the air had been mild compared to this. His heart had raced when he had found himself trapped by the Head Hunters, but his hand had been ever steady. Now he held his right arm out before him and saw it shaking.

He had instructions down to the letter. When he entered the room where King George was, he was to walk ten paces to the center of the room, turn left for thirty paces, and then bow before the monarch.

The doors were opened and an official nodded to him. He pulled himself together for the supreme test of his courage —this airman who had shot down forty-seven of his enemies —and in he went. He made the middle of the room all right, but when he turned for the thirty paces, his boots began to squeak.

"I was more frightened, actually, at that moment," he told me, "than at any time during the entire war."

The King smiled understandingly. Bishop stood at attention after he bowed, his face flushed. "Then some one started to read a long list of things I had done in the air," he told me. "It seemed like years until the reading stopped."

Then His Majesty was handed a plush pillow on which reposed the medals—the Victoria Cross, the Distinguished Service Order, and the Military Cross. Solemnly he hung them on the slight young man. "This," he said, "marks the first occasion on which I have bestowed all three of these honors on any one subject."

The King extended his right hand and shook Bishop's. The Canadian had been trying to think of something to say. He backed away—thirty squeaky paces—before he found his tongue. "Yes . . . sir," he gulped.

He had occasion later, when he met the King less formally, to tell him how nervous he had been. The King replied that he had been glad that he himself wasn't in Bishop's squeaky boots!

"A strange thing happened when I got out of the room after the investiture," the White Knight of Canada told me. "A man rushed up to me and plucked from my uniform the three decorations that His Majesty had pinned on me. Honestly, I thought I had been attacked by a robber right there in Buckingham Palace. He ran down the corridor, and I started after him. Then he stopped at a table. There were three boxes there. He put the medals in them and handed them to me, greatly astonished at my anxious behavior."

While waiting around London for further orders, Bishop was awarded a Bar to the D.S.O. and promoted to the rank of major. As he wondered if he was going to get back to the front, orders came to proceed to Canada. The stimulus of his presence was needed there.

It was a somewhat downhearted young major who took the boat train to Liverpool. Maybe the scrap would be over before he got a chance to hunt again. . . . But Margaret Burden waited in Toronto.

There were joyous times in the Dominion when public hero number one returned. He visited the Burden home in Toronto, he visited his family in Owen Sound. He went back to the Royal Military College at Kingston and laughed with instructors who had once been stern with him about his pranks. He attended public gatherings, against his will, because he knew that the ordeal that he went through would prove a tremendous stimulus to recruiting. He appeared on the platform of Massey Hall in Toronto with Lord North-cliffe, the great English publisher, and made a speech to a throng that packed the place, and a great new Red Cross drive was under way.

That was on October 14, 1917. Three days later Margaret Burden became Mrs. William Avery Bishop.

Back to England in January, 1918. He was attached to the School of Aircraft Gunnery in an instructional capacity, and hated it—although it wouldn't have been politic for him to say as much. His bride was with him, but he knew in his heart that he still had one last rendezvous to keep in the air. Mrs. Bishop knew it, too, and she uttered not one word against the plans he had in mind.

In the spring of 1918 the last great German offensives were under way. The British were driven back from Kemmel and the Somme. Sky combat became more vital than ever, observation more important; and both the Allies and the Germans had by this time developed still faster machines and produced them in still greater numbers. More than ever this was the place for Billy Bishop!

He got to the front again on May 22, in command of Eighty-five Squadron. But the War Office kept him grounded. They simply couldn't afford to risk him getting into the air. Why, even the well protected Baron von Richthofen had been killed, on April 21, by Roy Brown, a chap from Carleton Place in Bishop's home province of Ontario. If the R.F.C. boys had got through that ring of protection and shot down the Red Knight—indeed a fabulous hero in the earlier days of his career—it would certainly be possible for the enemy to get Bishop.

There was a boy from Royal Military College back in Kingston who had come up to Eighty-five Squadron—a strikingly courageous boy of twenty. Bishop took a great liking to him and taught him a lot of tricks—how to fight in-and-out, how to fall through a cloud as if you were done for, how to keep clear of traps.

The Flying Circus was playing as much havoc as ever with lame ducks and loners. The young man in command of it— Richthofen's successor—seemed extraordinarily fond of such one-sided fighting. His name was Hermann Goering.

Well, one day Goering and his pals got the kid from R.M.C. Bishop didn't see red. He didn't see at all. He was blind with rage. He went to a superior officer and announced quietly, *"Mister, I am flying again."*

His ship took to the skies and sped to the German lines. He dropped a note to Goering. He doesn't care to discuss its contents today, but we can draw on our imaginations. Goering didn't answer. That only made Bishop more furious—and he set out on a lone carnival of destruction that even to this day remains without a parallel in the history of aerial combat.

Billy Bishop winged through the blue like a thing possessed, flouting the Grim Reaper not once but a dozen times an hour, flying and fighting from dawn almost uninterruptedly until darkness. Witnesses to what he did in those ten days— witnesses on both sides of the lines—thought their eyes were deceiving them.

He began operations by plunging from above into a formation of six Head Hunters, flying in layers of two, three thousand feet apart. He knocked off one of the top pair and sent the other one away, scared and riddled, then roared down and repeated on the second pair.

His blue eyes narrowed as he plunged down farther. The two remaining Head Hunters were now streaking for the German lines. A sixty-mile gale was blowing in that direction. He would have to buck it to get back. Well, what of that? He caught one of the fleeing ships and shot its tail off.

The figure alongside of his name on the blackboard jumped from 47 to 50 when he came in.

He writes to his wife, back in London:

I feel like a picture I once saw, "On the eve of battle." We rather expect a good push from the Hun sometime tomorrow, and I've just been stirring the squadron into a suitable state of readiness. . . . I intended writing you . . . but I'm ashamed to say I forgot all about it until too late. . . . Margaret, my machine, my new one is a wonder. It fairly tears through the air. Tonight just to celebrate it I shot down a Pfalz in flames from 17,500 ft. There were four of them and I was so pleased to see a Hun again . . . that I just had to try my guns on them. Sure enough down they went and one of them in flames. 'Twas a merry sight withal. I'm so glad you're taking painting lessons . . .

He searched the skies for Goering. The newspapers of to-day bear witness to the fact that he never found him. But he found others—51, 52, 53, 54. And others—55, 56, 57, 58, 59, 60, 61.

Still others—62, 63, 64, 65, and 66.

He wouldn't eat. He fought sleep. Time was fleeting. He knew this wouldn't last forever. Afraid for himself? Hell, no! Afraid of the War Office. They'd crack down on him before long now.

67.

He doesn't remember the details himself. Anyway, one scrap's much like another. The other fellow gets you—or you get him.

He denies this tale today because he's a good soldier and believes in discipline. But men who knew him tell me that when he got the bad news—orders to return to England and a post in the Air Ministry, where he'd be safe and an inspiration to others—he clenched his teeth and said, "Oh for one more fight in the air!"

Whether or not he had those official orders in his pocket, the fact remains that he went up, that last day at the front, and bagged five. He came in disappointed.

"I really didn't get five," he told me. "I really got three. Two crashed into each other."

The greatest flyer of them all stepped out of his combat

ship for the last time. Twenty-five machines in ten days—five
of them in one day. And a living legend left the front.

When the war ended, William Avery Bishop of Owen
Sound was the possessor of virtually every medal for valor
within the gift of the British and French governments. Even
the Germans sought him out after the war. In 1928 a
flyers' association in Berlin, of which Hermann Goering was
a member, feted him and made him an honorary member.

He went into business after the war. He is now vice-
president of the McColl Frontenac Oil Company. Marshal
and Mrs. Bishop have two children—Arthur, aged sixteen,
the only Canadian godson of H. R. H. the Duke of Con-
naught, and Marise, fourteen, goddaughter of Princess Marie
Louise.

The Ministry of National Defense made him Honorary
Air Marshal. And then the new war this last September. I
happened to be in Montreal when the Four Horsemen rode
again in Europe. And so, when Billy Bishop was appointed
Marshal of the Royal Canadian Air Force, I heard with my
own ears and felt the meaning of the words that echoed
throughout the Dominion: *"Bishop flies again!"*

Chivalry in the Air

BY LT. COL. WILLIAM A. BISHOP

[*Editor's Note: Colonel Bishop was the Allies' greatest ace of the war. A native of Ontario, he was known as the White Knight of Canada in answer to his great rival, Baron Manfred von Richthofen, the Red Knight of Germany. Bishop was the victor of more than a hundred sky combats, with an official record of seventy-two enemy planes destroyed. Awarded all of the highest British decorations—the Victoria Cross, the Distinguished Service Order and Bar, the Military Cross, the Distinguished Flying Cross—he also received the French Legion of Honor and the Croix de Guerre with Palm.*]

◎ ◎ ◎ ◎ ◎ ◎ ◎ ◎ ◎

CHIVALRY! Of course it existed! The bitterness and hatred between the armies and navies engaged in the War, as well as the intense feeling of the civilians, was not present in the Air Forces of the countries involved. In its place was a healthy respect for and interest in the opposing flying men.

This was of course due to several definite causes. Since the Wrights captured the air there has always been a great atmosphere of romance surrounding it. The War enhanced this. The flying men themselves felt the thrill of conquering a new element and their interest in the development of aviation was always at concert pitch. They liked their work; they admired their comrades; and in fairness admired equally

73

their foes. There were no sordid points of contact between the opposing pilots, such as surrounded the troops on the ground. They met in the cold clear air, highly trained, expensively equipped, in battles where their own skill and the quality of their equipment were the two vital factors in deciding their fate. It was a battle of skill and wits, free from animosity of any kind, a game more than a war; and of the hundreds of times I have seen pilots return to their aërodrome badly shot about—and so often having barely escaped with their lives—I have never heard remarks of any kind other than of great admiration for their opponents.

This feeling almost of friendship did exist, and on both sides of the lines. Of this I have ample proof. But to understand it, it is necessary to appreciate that we did—I am now speaking as a fighting pilot—truly regard our work as a game and not as war. Although we always aimed to kill the pilot, we did that as the surest way of destroying an enemy machine, and not with the thought of shooting a man. It was as impersonal as a hard-fought battle on the gridiron or in the boxing ring, and the Germans and Austrians had the same spirit.

From the beginning of air fighting, notes were dropped at great personal risk, telling the fate of members of opposing forces who had failed to return to their own lines, and in many cases these were accompanied by messagse of admiration for the skill and bravery of the missing airman.

When Boelcke, the great German ace, who was Richthofen's leader and teacher, was killed in a collision, British machines flew over to Cambrai, where he was stationed, and dropped wreaths with notes attached, which read:

To the memory of Captain Boelcke, our brave and chivalrous foe, from the British Flying Corps
and
To the officers of the German Flying Corps and Services at the front—
We hope you will find this wreath but we are sorry it is so late in coming. The weather has prevented us from sending it earlier. We mourn with his relatives and friends—we all recognise his bravery. Please give our

kind regards to Captain Evans and Lieutenant Long
of the Morane Squadron.

> (signed)—J. Seeman Greene, Lieutenant.

Nor did this feeling exist only while in the air. On the
ground when those rare occasions came for us to meet our
opponents it was most marked. These opportunities only
occurred of course when a prisoner was taken. In nearly all
cases, except when they were wounded, we entertained these
prisoners in our messes, and great care was taken that they
were treated as gentlemen and guests, and not as prisoners.
True, of course, that this pleasure was allowed us in the
hopes that we could get information of a technical nature
from them, but that was not our attitude when they arrived
in our midst. The first move was to introduce them to the
various officers; the second to offer them enough cigarettes
and drinks to quiet their nerves and lessen the heartache of
being captured.

In my own squadron, we have had on occasions officers
for several days before passing them on. Although I have
seen them so nervous on arrival that in one case an officer
jumped to his feet and saluted the mess waiter who was
offering him a cocktail, usually at the end of an hour they
were comparatively at ease. When the time came to part, they
were always sent away properly supplied with clothing and
such small comforts as we could give them to help in the
dull prospect ahead of a long rest in a prison camp.

In many cases, prisoners on both sides of the lines were
allowed to write notes or letters to their relatives or friends
in their squadron telling that they were safe and well, or
wounded, as the case might be, and these messages were
dropped by their captors at some spot over the opposing lines
where they were certain to reach their destination. Sometimes
as well, messages would be dropped asking for special clothing or equipment which the prisoner did not have with him.

This was often necessary, as pilots were extremely careless
about their dress when flying, and I recall that in the summer
of 1917, when it was very hot, we in Sixty Squadron used
to do our dawn patrols in our pyjamas, with nothing over
them but flying boots and flying coats. It is not hard, therefore, to picture the predicament in which a pilot found him-

self when captured by the enemy so inappropriately attired!
It was a serious matter for him too, as it was necessary for
him to be properly dressed, in order to prove his rank and
receive the treatment due to it. I think that we on our side
saw the humor of these situations much more than the Germans did, although they seemed equally willing to help out
the unfortunate prisoner.

Here is a typical case in point. Early in 1918, Lieutenant
Jerrard of Sixty-six Squadron, operating in Italy over the
Piave, was shot down in a tremendous fight near an Austrian
aërodrome, during which he sacrificed himself to save some
of the other members of his squadron. This was such a
gallant show that he was awarded the Victoria Cross for it.
When he landed on the ground, however, the Germans found
him very improperly dressed for a long stay in a prison
camp. For one thing, he was not wearing his Sam Browne
belt, which to them was the main distinction between an
officer and a private. It was therefore vital for him to get
one, in order that he would go to an officers' and not to a
privates' prison camp. With this in view, his captors flew back
to a British aërodrome and dropped a note written in French
explaining Lieutenant Jerrard's predicament, and also enclos-
ing an uncensored note from him to his parents, which they
asked the British Squadron to forward.

As soon as this note was received at his Squadron, two
bundles of clothes were made up—including a Sam Browne
belt, shoes, socks, cigarettes and everything that he might require. Aëroplanes then left carrying these bundles, and notes
of condolence, which they dropped over the aërodrome where
the fight had occurred. It is significant to point out that on
the way from the British aërodrome to the German aërodrome these machines were under hot and intense fire from
the Austrian anti-aircraft batteries and to note that from the
moment they dropped the bundles and started their rush for
home not a shot was fired at them, nor did any Austrian
machine attempt to attack them. This instance, to my mind,
is most conclusive proof that chivalry did exist between the
Air Arms.

I have often heard it argued that no friendly spirit could
possibly exist between the fighting air forces, when it is ac-
knowledged that both sides have fired upon balloonists who

were escaping from their balloons in parachutes. And my
answer to this is, that the difference—although a very subtle
one—was nevertheless quite distinct in our minds. The first
time I heard of balloonists being shot at while descending in
their parachutes was in the Spring of 1917 at the Battle of
Vimy Ridge. On that day two Germans destroyed five of our
balloons, and in several cases stayed to fire at the balloonists while they were parachuting to earth.

We had at this time received strict instructions that when
attacking balloons we were to concentrate upon destroying
the personnel, as this was more important than the balloon
itself—the reason being that trained balloonists were much
harder to replace than the balloon, a substitute for which
could be in operation in a few hours. I consider, therefore,
that those cases, where observers were fired upon while
parachuting to earth, were simply operations of war carried
out, in almost all instances, under specific orders. As regards
parachute descents from aëroplanes, these were extremely
rare during the War. I have never heard of a man escaping
from an aëroplane in a parachute who was fired upon by
an enemy machine, and I cannot conceive any pilot doing it.

In fights, machines have frequently been forced to land
although they have not actually been shot down. The victor
in these circumstances would always if possible fire at these
machines upon the ground, in the hope of completely destroying them, but it was seldom, if ever, that he would fire on
the pilot if he was running away from his machine. I have
never heard of this being done, but I have often heard of episodes where the escaping aviator had been waved to by his
victor and left unharmed.

This business of waving to each other was not confined to
episodes like the above, and has actually occurred many times
in the air. A most interesting example of it was experienced
by Major Maclaren, D.S.O., M.C., D.F.C., a Canadian ace
who was accredited with forty-eight enemy machines destroyed.

One day, while flying over the German lines, he engaged
an enemy two-seater, and after considerable manoeuvring got
himself within close range of the enemy machine, and in
such a position that he could not be fired upon by the

enemy observer. Taking aim, he pressed his triggers, but to his annoyance his guns refused to work.

Pulling out of the fight for a few minutes, he thought he had readjusted them, and after some more manoeuvring placed himself in the same position as before. Again he pressed his triggers, but no shot came from his guns. Feeling his ammunition chutes, he discovered that both belts were broken. By this time he had lost his perfect position of being in his enemy's blind spot, but to his astonishment, he saw that the German was not firing at him. He flew closer, and almost alongside, and saw that the observer was standing with his machine gun pointing up into the air, away from him. Suddenly the observer waved to him, and moved his gun up and down, signalling that he had no more ammunition. Maclaren then flew in as close to him as he possibly could without colliding and waved back at him. The German pilot and the observer both returned the greeting, and they parted the best of friends.

Shortly before the Battle of Arras in 1917, there was operating in front of Monchy almost daily a German two-seater which always aroused our greatest admiration. On several occasions, when we got to close quarters, we noticed that the observer of this machine was so big that he could hardly fit into the cockpit. He was, however, very quick in moving about and a good shot, although his pilot was far from being a good pilot. We took such an interest in this huge fat German that he was affectionately nicknamed in our Squadron "The Flying Pig." After one fight in which he escaped by getting down too low to the ground for us to follow—but during which he had put up a very stout-hearted performance—we decided that so far as our Squadron was concerned, he had earned immunity, and we forbade any pilot to shoot to kill him. In other words, we began to look upon him as our own pet mascot. To our great horror, ten days later, however, a new young pilot, who had been informed of the story of the Flying Pig but who in his enthusiasm did not recognise him, attacked and shot him down. We held that night, in our Squadron Mess, a dinner in his honor, and drank his health in the same way as we would one of our own pilots.

There are instances and instances of things of this kind

which were almost daily occurrences, and although they were frowned upon at Headquarters as not being in keeping with the general policy of conducting a war, in which bitterness and hatred seemed to be as necessary as machine guns and ammunition, this good feeling could not be quelled.

Two instances of people being really bad shot about and bearing no resentment come to my mind here. One is of Major Keith Caldwell, a New Zealander, and the other of myself. In both cases we had very narrow escapes but felt nothing but admiration for our opponents.

In Caldwell's case, I was standing on our aërodrome in France in May, 1917, when I saw him return from the front line, and very gingerly indeed—for him—land his little Nieuport fighter. He taxied slowly up to the hangar and I strolled over to ask him his luck; before I reached him, however, he was out of his machine and striding away towards the officers' mess. I saw the Flight Sergeant follow him, asking for instructions about his machine and I heard a very surly reply from Caldwell—"Burn the bloody thing"—as he continued walking away muttering to himself.

More than curious, I went to look at the machine and found it riddled with bullets. To my astonishment too, the bullets had all come from behind and had evidently in different groups pierced the machine on both sides of the pilot's seat, barely missing him. My surprise was great because "Grid," as we called him, was a wonderful pilot and an extremely courageous fighter.

Still more curious, I was about to follow him to the mess when a telephone message came through from a front line observation post telling of a great duel between a German and a Nieuport which had started at 12,000 feet and been fought all the way down to the ground. The German had the best of it all the way, and all the skill of Caldwell, which was perfect, could not shake the enemy off his tail.

So to the mess I went to hear more particulars. On the way several pilots met me and said, "Don't speak to Grid, he is in a terrific temper." I went up to him, and after three or four questions to which he didn't pay any attention, I said, "That must have been a great pilot you were fighting. How did it happen and who was it?"

He looked up and grinned—"Hell's own fury in an Albatros Scout!" Here was no bitterness—just praise!

The other incident occurred to me in a fight with
Richthofen—

Richthofen was, as I say, at his best at this time, and one
afternoon, flying with my Squadron Commander, Major
Scott, and seeing four German fighting machines, I led him
in to attack them, arriving at approximately the same height
at which they were flying. The next few minutes were almost
the most hectic of my life, and gave me the biggest surprise
I ever got. Three of the Germans cleared off to one side and
the leader (Richthofen) took the two of us on. We at that
time had both shot down a number of Germans . . . I think
my score was around twenty and Major Scott's about twelve,
and we were beginning to feel that we knew more about the
game than anybody else, and therein lies the humor of this
fight. . . . Richthofen promptly gave us the rudest shock we
could possibly have had. His three friends stood off to one
side in case one of us tried to get away. He at the beginning
of the fight got almost on my tail—which is the ideal place
to be—and the only way I could avoid being shot down was
to turn immediately across him, giving him the most difficult
shot in air-fighting, as I was flying directly across at right
angles to him at roughly 100 miles an hour. He fired seven
bullets in one burst, all of which ripped through the back of
my seat and through the folds of my flying coat. The most
beautiful shooting I have ever seen. This didn't make me feel
any too happy, and, worse still, a few seconds later he had me
in a position where the only thing I could do was to give
him the same shot again. I suppose he had seen his tracer
bullets going a matter of a few inches too far back, and this
time allowed for more deflection and another burst of his
bullets came right through, cutting my instrument board and
instruments to pieces. He had in the meantime also considerably damaged Major Scott, and had shot through part
of his engine, with the result that it was operating at reduced
power, making it very difficult for him to fly. On the other
hand, Richthofen was not having it all his own way; after
that second burst I made up my mind that he was not going
to get another crack at me, and I managed a few seconds
later to get almost directly behind him, and I opened up with

my gun as hard as I could. I thought I had shot him down,
as he immediately dived straight towards the ground, and
unquestionably I must have shot his machine up very
badly, as I was firing at him from less than forty yards'
range. However, our attention was taken by the three other
Germans, who attacked immediately, and I do not know what
the result would have been in the fight with them, because at
that moment another flight of aëroplanes appeared a few
thousand feet above, at which the Germans cleared off—
and so did we!

We then recognised the flight above as being British and
they escorted us home. The last stages of the fight took a few
seconds only, and I looked down in the hopes of seeing
Richthofen crash, only to see him about 4,000 feet below
flatten out and fly towards his aërodrome. He had nearly
finished my young life, but no thought other than admiration
was in my mind as we flew home.

The burial of von Richthofen behind the British lines in
1918 was a just and fitting tribute to the wonderful career
of that great German soldier. He was buried with the fullest
of military honors, and not an aviator in the whole of our
flying forces but felt a real pang of sorrow that such a great
career should be ended—although it goes without saying that
the fact that he had been eliminated from the German forces
was to us all a tremendous relief. However (although he
probably would not have wished it himself), it would have
been to us much more satisfactory if he could have been
captured and his life spared.

I have met since the War many pilots of the German Flying Corps and these meetings have confirmed my feeling of
admiration for them and their good sportsmanship.

A few years ago I was entertained in Berlin by a large
number of these German war pilots . . . men against whom
my Squadron and I had frequently been engaged in mortal
combat. Their reception of me is something which I shall
never forget, and an experience which I shall always look
back on with great pride and satisfaction.

At this luncheon we discussed in the frankest terms all
the serious and amusing sides of our experiences. I have
been told so often that these flying men—brave and fine
fellows—were usually lacking in a real sense of humor, but

I found the reverse to be the case. For instance, the first thing we did was to have a group photograph taken underneath a portrait of the Kaiser!

All round the room in which we were lunching were paintings and drawings of fights in the air, and when the time came for me to reply to their toast, I referred to these pictures. I pointed out that, interesting as they were, to me they did not seem to be technically correct. Many good pictures there were which I had seen of fighting in the air, but never like these, which all showed Allied machines being shot down by German pilots, and I told them that in so far as I knew such a thing had never occurred. They appreciated my point but disagreed with me.

Amongst the points on which I was curious and questioned them was by what nickname they referred to us. I explained that we always called them "Huns," it being the most objectionable-sounding name we could think of. Their answer was quick and to the point. They told me they had no special nickname for us, but merely called us "Englishers," as they considered that bad enough!

This was the spirit in which we sat down together, and this was the spirit in which we fought our battles in the air.

Rickenbacker —
The Ace of Aces of the American Expeditionary Force

BY GEN. WILLIAM MITCHELL

[*Editor's Note: General "Billy" Mitchell was the commander of American air forces in 1918. Even before the war began he was one of the few men in the country who urged the development of American military aviation, but after the war his zeal in this cause only succeeded in antagonizing the old guard officers of the army and navy. He was court-martialed in 1925 and demoted to Colonel. He then resigned his commission and died ten years later, shortly after the Military Affairs Committee of the House of Representatives voted not to reinstate his name to the list of retired army officers. During World War II his predictions about the use of air power were completely vindicated, and in 1945 the Senate voted to grant him posthumously the Congressional Medal of Honor and promoted him to the rank of Major General.*]

◎ ◎ ◎ ◎ ◎ ◎ ◎ ◎ ◎

AN ace in aviation is one who has shot down five enemy airplanes in air battles, which must be definitely established by the testimony of two or more witnesses, so as to leave no doubt as to the occurrences. The word "ace" is applied loosely now to flyers who make a spectacular trip almost anywhere, but it is a misnomer. Only those who have dared to participate in the world's most dangerous combat and have come out victorious deserve to be called such.

Our American pilots in the World War entered into full combat almost immediately with men who had been fighting for three years, and during the latter part of the war they were pitted against the very best airmen in the German service. At the time of the Armistice, Edward V. Rickenbacker, commanding the Ninety-fourth Pursuit Squadron of the First Pursuit Group, was the American ace of aces. This article is a short account of some of his service as I observed it.

In order to appreciate the conditions that obtained in Europe when we entered the war, it is necessary to understand what the feeling was in France and Great Britain at that time. The spring of 1917 opened ominously for the Allies. For almost three years the Germans had been in occupation of French territory. They had destroyed the Russians' mammoth army and taken the sting out of the Italians. The Slavonic states and Roumania were about to be brought into complete subjection. The Germans' Turkish allies were being resuscitated and reorganized.

The British and French had battered their brains out against the German concrete defenses on the Western Front, and it was expected that as soon as the warmth of spring made campaigning easier the whole weight of Germany and her allies would be hurled in against the French army. The only possible aid to the French would be from the United States and, even at that, it was problematical whether we could send assistance in sufficient strength before the terrible catastrophe might occur.

It was under these circumstances, upon the declaration of war on April 6, 1917, that I joined our small group of officers in Paris, having hurried there from Spain, where I had been on an inspection trip. The French army was about to attack. Old "Papa" Joffre, who had saved the French at the Battle of the Marne, had been removed from the command of the French armies because he was opposed to an offensive. He knew that if an attack in force were made against the Germans at that time, it would spell ruin. His strategy was to keep on "nibbling" at the Germans, forcing them to attack, until such time as their strength would be so diminished as to warrant a counteroffensive. But the politicians gained the upper hand, and General Nivelle, who was committed to the offensive, was placed in command.

The Germans knew it was coming. The French army was their most dangerous opponent. If they could destroy the French army, the war would be virtually over. The French and British armies were supposed to attack at the same time, but the Germans had laid waste a strip of land about twenty miles wide in front of the British. All the roads were bombed, the bridges destroyed, buildings demolished, even the trees killed, and the whole area was so utterly devastated that it was impossible for the British army to move across it in time to take part in the April attacks.

But the French went ahead and attacked anyway, and lost over 100,000 men in three weeks without budging the Germans.

I was with the Fourth French army that was making the attack. One evening I was seated at dinner with General Pétain, then commanding the group of armies that were attacking. The conversation turned to what we Americans could do during the war. I said that I knew we could furnish good aviators, to which General Pétain replied that he thought so also, as our supply of men suitable to become pilots was almost inexhaustible, but that theirs was almost used up. He thought we could furnish good heavy artillery, because this would be used at a considerable distance behind the enemy front and would not be subject to heavy casualties, and could be manned largely by mechanics who would not have to have the military foundation and discipline required of combat troops.

He asked me if I thought we could dispatch a conscript army to France and have it fight in offensive battles against a powerful enemy such as the Germans. In answer, I asked him if he thought that, were the United States locked in a death struggle with a Pacific power in our western states, France could send a conscript army to help us. He replied, "Probably no." I then told him I thought we could send a conscript army, and if they succeeded in reaching France they would do well after a certain time. It had been our history that when the spirit of the American people was moved they would attempt anything.

I talked with some of the peasants in the Champagne country behind the positions where the terrific battles were taking place during April. They said, "We hear you Americans have come into the war to help us, but what can you do? At best you can only prolong the struggle, and in that case we will not be able to get as good terms from the enemy as we can now, because we will not be so strong. The politicians bring on the wars, the people in the cities make the money out of them, but we in the country are the ones that fight the enemy and lose all our men. We are tired of doing it."

Often I went out from the middle of Paris to Le Bourget airdrome on the northern outskirts, where my airplane was kept. To reach the field, I had to go through the slaughterhouse district, the "tough part of town." I often saw men haranguing crowds, vehemently denouncing the war. The *bonnet rouge*, signal of revolution in France, was carried through the streets.

Of course, feeling in the interior of a country is never the same as it is in the armies at the front. The French armies, in spite of their terrific casualties, maintained their cohesion and fighting spirit as has always been their custom, although the seeds of mutiny appeared in no uncertain form in some places. Conditions were equally bad in the British Isles. Food was very scarce and the people were pessimistic.

I immediately set out to do everything possible to prepare for the rapid organization of our aviation when our men should come, and in this I was assisted in every way possible by the French army and their civil departments. Gradually we heard about what was happening in the United States—how the whole country was flying to arms and making preparations for war in a serious way. Then we heard that General Pershing was to command the American troops, and in the latter part of June he reached Paris amid the acclaim of the people. With him as aëronautical officer was Major Townsend F. Dodd, an able, brave, and resourceful officer. As his adjutant he had brought Captain Birdseye Lewis, and with them came a few soldiers and clerks.

In a few days General Pershing had decided on our

organization and put me in charge of our aviation. My plans received his hearty approval. I decided to make a trip through the sector which our armies were to occupy and definitely establish the points for our future operations.

A few American automobiles had arrived and Captain Lewis secured two Packards. In these Major Dodd and I started into the northern part of France. With me were a chauffeur, Flake, and two Frenchmen, a Captain Raulin and an adjutant from the French army named Boyriven. Major Dodd had with him Captain Lewis and a tall, muscularly built young man with prominent features and big hands, driving the car.

After we had inspected and decided on the sites for several of our air stations, we drove through the city of Toul and into Nancy. At Toul the roar of artillery could be heard in the distance and a few airplanes were overhead. We reached Nancy as darkness was settling over the town, obtained billets, then went to the Café Walter in the beautiful Stanislas Square for our dinner. We sat long over the meal, discussing our problems, and just as we were nearly through there was a sudden sound of sirens through the town, announcing the *alerte* for a raid of German bombing planes. Everyone was ordered into the caves or wine cellars. I wished to see as much of this raid as I could, but did not want to be in the center of the city because I had tried that a couple of months before at Châlons, where an airplane bomb had exploded across the street from me, though I had escaped with only a bruise in the leg from a shell fragment.

I inquired as to where we could see the bombardment of the town safely and to the best advantage, and was told to take the road to Pont St. Vincent, where we could ascend a hill about a mile out of the city which overlooked the whole place.

We departed with all speed, and as we ascended the hill we could see the searchlights shining all over the city, and the bursting projectiles from anti-aircraft guns, and could hear the whir of the German airplane engines. The Germans appeared to pay little attention to the anti-aircraft artillery; they came straight on for their objectives. Suddenly there was a terrific explosion and a great flash on the far side of the city, then in rapid succession another and another. The

searchlights continued to sweep the air and the artillery
fired incessantly, but still the airplanes circled above.

There were three more great explosions, followed by flames
that ascended to one hundred feet or more. It looked as
though the railroad station had been hit. We could hear
the fire alarm and the fire engines going through the streets.
The sound of the airplane engines faded away and we returned to the city to learn what had happened. The fire
was still raging in the vicinity of the railroad station and
many houses had caught fire; in fact, two or three city
blocks were in flames.

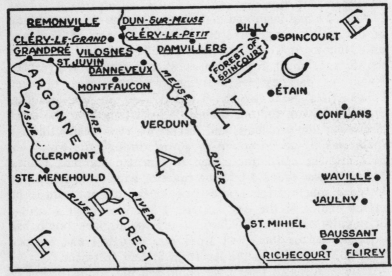

*Showing the localities where Captain Rickenbacker won most
of his victories. Their names are underscored.*

The first airplane, flying at about 1,000 feet, had attacked
a factory in the city which made projectiles for artillery,
and occupied almost a whole block. The first bomb had hit
the street in front of the factory, demolishing a lot of the
wall and breaking all the windows. The second and third
bombs had dropped squarely within the building, demolishing the whole thing. No more projectiles were made in that
factory during the war.

The second airplane had attacked the railroad station,
into which a trainload of gasoline and petroleum was just

RICKENBACKER'S OFFICIAL VICTORIES

In this list it is interesting to note that Rickenbacker brought down four balloons and twenty-one planes, and that of the latter twelve were Fokkers. These were designed by the Dutch airplane builder A. H. G. Fokker, who—Holland being neutral in the war—offered his plans first to the British, French, and Russian governments, none of which accepted them. Then they were offered to Germany, and the Fokker ships proved one of the Germans' most effective war weapons. Now Fokker is in the United States and Rickenbacker is employed by the Fokker Aircraft Corporation as vice president and director of sales—marketing the machines he once shot down. The list has been checked by the War Department records of his victories.

Date (1918)	Type of Plane	Region	Time	Altitude (Meters)
April 29	Albatros	Baussant	6:10 P.M.	2,000
May 17	Albatros	Richecourt	6:24 A.M.	4,500
May 22	Albatros	Flirey	9:12 A.M.	4,500
May 28	Albatros two-seater	Bois de Raté	9:35 A.M.	2,500
May 30	Albatros two-seater	Jaulny	7:38 A.M.	4,500
Sept. 14	Fokker	Villey Waville	8:15 A.M.	3,000
Sept. 15	Fokker	Boie de Warville	8:10 A.M.	4,000
Sept. 25	Fokker	Billy	8:40 A.M.	3,000
Sept. 25	Halberstadt	Forêt de Spincourt	8:50 A.M.	2,000
Sept. 26	Fokker	Damvillers	6:00 A.M.	1,500
Sept. 28	Balloon	Sivry-sur-Meuse	6:00 A.M.	100
Oct. 1	Balloon	Puxieux	7:30 P.M.	On ground
Oct. 2	Fokker	Vilosnes	5:40 P.M.	1,000
Oct. 2	Halberstadt	Montfaucon	5:30 P.M.	600
Oct. 3	L. V. G.	Danneveux	5:07 P.M.	600
Oct. 3	Rumpler	Cléry-le-Grand	4:40 P.M.	500
Oct. 9	Balloon	Dun-sur-Meuse	5:52 P.M.	On ground
Oct. 10	Fokker	Cléry-le-Petit	3:52 P.M.	800
Oct. 10	Fokker	Cléry-le-Petit	3:52 P.M.	600
Oct. 22	Fokker	Cléry-le-Petit	3:55 P.M.	1,200
Oct. 23	Fokker	Petit-le-Grand	5:05 P.M.	600
Oct. 27	Fokker	Carré Ferme, Grandpré	2:50 P.M.	2,000
Oct. 27	Fokker	Bois-de-Money	3:05 P.M.	3,000
Oct. 30	Balloon	Remonville	4:40 P.M.	On ground
Oct. 30	Fokker	St. Juvin	4:35 P.M.	200

coming. One bomb had hit the station; another had hit the
train, setting it on fire and scattering the flames all over
that part of town. The third bomb had hit a group of buildings and set them on fire. This attack of two airplanes using
bombs of about 200 pounds in weight had caused a tremendous amount of damage and an order from the authorities for the evacuation of the city by its civilian population.

As we were leaving the city on the following morning,
wending our way through the hills back toward Neufchâteau, the engine in my motor car suddenly spluttered
and stopped. My chauffeur got out, lifted the hood, and
started looking for the trouble, but although he worked over
it a long time he was unable to repair it. Dodd suggested
that his driver come up and see what he could do. So the
tall, lithe young man dived into the engine and in a moment
he had removed the whole carburetor assembly which with
the old twin-six Packard engine was almost as big as the
engine itself. He found that the needle valve had bent, and
in less time than it takes to tell he cleaned it, put it back,
and had the engine going. I had never seen a man do anything so quickly with a gasoline engine, or who knew more
about what he was doing.

That day at luncheon I asked Dodd where he obtained his
chauffeur, and he replied that Lewis had got him in the
United States to go along with us. He was a champion
automobile racing driver, Dodd told me, and had proved
himself to be one of the best soldiers he had ever known.
His name was Rickenbacker.

From that time on, this man interested me greatly. Any
job that he was given was done in the best possible manner.
He was never late and was always well turned out, neat in
his personal appearance, punctilious and gentlemanly. We
gave him many missions to execute which required judgment
and discretion, and although in a strange environment he
kept doing better and better.

I found that he had been in England when war was declared, under contract with one of the automobile companies there to organize an automobile racing team. Upon
our declaration of war he immediately returned to the
United States. However, on account of his German name

and parentage he was suspected by the English of being a German spy and was followed and watched across the ocean and the United States by British agents, until they were convinced that he was not one. Rickenbacker was not aware of this until one of the Scotland Yard men approached him in San Francisco and told him he had enjoyed the trip through America.

Rickenbacker sailed for France with the first American contingent, on the boat with General Pershing and his party, and landed in France on June 9, 1917.

One day I was standing talking to some French officers opposite our aviation headquarters in Paris. I noticed Rickenbacker coming across the street toward me. He waited until I had concluded the conversation, then came up, saluted, and said he had permission from his commanding officer to speak to me. I asked him what he wanted and he said that he desired to fly and become a pilot, as that had been his overpowering ambition from the time he first went into the service. His familiarity with automobiles and motors and his experience as a racing driver would help him greatly, he believed. We were very short of good men on our staff at that time, but Rickenbacker's request so impressed me that I immediately sent him to the aviation school at Tours, where French instructors were teaching our men pending the organization of our own school at Issoudun.

Rickenbacker learned to fly in three weeks. He worked at it constantly and distinguished himself particularly in the upkeep of his engine, airplane, and armament. We were just organizing our school at Issoudun and Rickenbacker was made a lieutenant and engineering officer of the school.

In the spring of 1918 Rickenbacker joined the Ninety-fourth Squadron of the First Pursuit Group and was sent to the airdrome called Villeneuve, and then to the one at Epiez behind Epernay in the Champagne. Here the pursuit group was given the best instruction possible, particularly by Major Menard of the French pursuit aviation. While it did not enter into open combat on the front as an organization, individuals went with the French air squadrons and saw something of the combats. During the first part of April the Ninety-fourth Squadron, accompanied by the Ninety-fifth, arrived on the Toul airdrome and we were definitely

given a section of the front to defend. It was the first time
that an American air unit had been intrusted with an independent command. It marked the real birth of American
fighting air power.

Two days after the squadron's arrival, a patrol was sent
out over the front. It became separated, and on account of
the poor visibility two or three of the ships flew over the
ground held by the Germans—"Germany," as we called it.
Rickenbacker was a member of this patrol. They were sighted
by the Germans, who immediately sent up their ships to
engage them. As these German planes crossed the lines they
were reported by the French observation posts, who could
not see them but could hear their engines above the clouds.
We had on the Toul airdrome, available for a reserve, three
airplanes, piloted by Lieutenants Alan Winslow, Douglas
Campbell, and James Meissner. They were ordered to stand
by their ships, and in a moment word came from the observation post on Mont Mihiel that the German airplanes
were immediately above the city of Toul, where they could
not be seen from the ground on account of the low clouds.

Lieutenants Campbell and Winslow immediately took
the air, but Meissner could not start his motor.

As our men approached the cloud ceiling, two German
ships came out of it. The whole population of the city of
Toul was watching. Winslow immediately attacked and shot
down his plane, and Campbell followed suit. The German
planes came to the ground and the pilots were captured.
One was a man of long experience, with many victories to
his credit.

This was the first combat of an American organization
with the Germans and showed clearly the splendid training,
wonderful flying ability, and dash which our men possessed. The general commanding the French troops in that
area had the wrecks of the German airplanes brought in
and displayed in the public square of Toul, with a band
playing, so the people could see what the Americans had
done. It was a splendid omen of our success. Word spread
throughout the country of the prowess of the Americans, and
every pilot in our group was filled with a desire to emulate
Lieutenants Campbell and Winslow.

Rickenbacker landed on the airdrome shortly after this

had occurred. He had hoped to be the first man to shoot down a German airplane, and it made him doubly desirous of entering into combat at the earliest opportunity.

Lufbery, the American who had been in the French service, had greatly distinguished himself as a pursuit pilot and had seventeen victories to his credit. He had been taken into the American service and made a major and had joined the First Pursuit Group as a battle instructor, in which capacity he excelled. Rickenbacker talked to him constantly. I think Rickenbacker's training as a racing driver gave him an invaluable preparation for air fighting. A driver must watch every maneuver of his rivals, and think ahead of time about how to take the turns on the track, how another driver can be passed or blocked, and what the temperaments and personalities of the other contenders may be.

Besides, Rickenbacker was twenty-eight years old, in full vigor, and possessed of mature judgment. Some nations attempted to get very young men into the service and inculcate a spirit of the offensive into them so they would take all sorts of risks, with the hope that they would account for two or three of the enemy before they were killed themselves. Others taught their pilots too great caution. But in Rickenbacker we had the rare combination of sound judgment and fighting spirit, quick thinking, and great manual dexterity in handling his craft. He wished to close with his enemy in mortal combat, in which no quarter was asked or given and where failure meant death in a burning torch in the air or crushed against the earth beneath a fallen plane.

Rickenbacker participated in a good many combats with other pilots before actually getting an enemy airplane to his credit. This probably was a good thing, because, given a calculating mind such as Rickenbacker's, it afforded him an opportunity to think over the occurrences which he had witnessed and analyze their efforts. Many a good pilot obtained a victory over an enemy too easily, shooting one down on his first encounter, with the result that he became careless and was soon destroyed himself.

At this period we were "making" our American aviation and I was watching the work of each pilot with great care and intense interest, because from this group of truly won-

derful young men I would have to select commanding officers
for many of the future fighting groups of our aviation.

Rickenbacker obtained his first victory over the enemy on
April 29, 1918. He had gone out with Captain James Norman
Hall, an exceptional pilot and remarkable air fighter. I quote
from Rickenbacker's own account of this first victory:

There was a scout coming toward us from north of
Pont-à-Mousson. It was at about our altitude. I knew
it was a Hun the moment I saw it, for it had the
familiar lines of their new Pfalz. Moreover, my confidence in James Norman Hall was such that I knew
he couldn't make a mistake. And he was still climbing into the sun, carefully keeping his position between its glare and the oncoming fighting plane. I
clung as closely to Hall as I could. The Hun was
steadily approaching us, unconscious of his danger, for
we were full in the sun.

With the first downward dive of Jimmy's machine
I was by his side. We had at least a thousand feet
advantage over the enemy, and we were two to one
numerically. He might outdive our machines, for the
Pfalz is a famous diver, while our faster climbing
Nieuports had a droll little habit of shedding their
fabric when plunged too furiously through the air.
The Boche hadn't a chance to outfly us. His only
salvation would be in a dive towards his own lines.

These thoughts passed through my mind in a flash
and I instantly determined upon my tactics. While Hall
went in for his attack I would keep my altitude and
get a position the other side of the Pfalz, to cut off
his retreat.

No sooner had I altered my line of flight than the
German pilot saw me leave the sun's rays. Hall was
already halfway to him when he stuck up his nose
and began furiously climbing to the upper ceiling. I
let him pass me and found myself on the other side
just as Hall began firing. I doubt if the Boche had
seen Hall's Nieuport at all.

Surprised by discovering this new antagonist, Hall,
ahead of him, the Pfalz immediately abandoned all

idea of a battle and banking around to the right
started for home, just as I had expected him to do.
In a trice I was on his tail. Down, down we sped
with throttles both full open. Hall was coming on
somewhere in my rear. The Boche had no heart for
evolutions or maneuvers. He was running like a scared
rabbit, as I had run from Campbell. I was gaining
upon him every instant, and had my sights trained
dead upon his seat before I fired my first shot.

At 150 yards I pressed my triggers. The tracer
bullets cut a streak of living fire into the rear of the
Pfalz's tail. Raising the nose of my aëroplane slightly,
the fiery streak lifted itself like the stream of water
pouring from a garden hose. Gradually it settled into
the pilot's seat. The swerving of the Pfalz course indicated that its rudder no longer was held by a directing hand. At 2,000 feet above the enemy's lines I
pulled up my headlong dive and watched the enemy
machine continuing on its course. Curving slightly to
the left the Pfalz circled a little to the south and the
next minute crashed on to the ground just at the
edge of the woods a mile inside their own lines. I
had brought down my first enemy aëroplane and had
not been subjected to a single shot!

Hall was immediately beside me. He was evidently
as pleased as I was over our success, for he danced
his machine about in incredible maneuvers. And then
I realized that old friend Archy was back on the job.
We were not two miles away from the German anti-
aircraft batteries and they put a furious bombardment
of shrapnel all about us. I was quite ready to call it
a day and go home, but Captain Hall deliberately returned to the barrage and entered it with me at his
heels. Machine guns and rifle fire from the trenches
greeted us and I do not mind admitting that I got out
quickly the way I came in without any unnecessary
delay, but Hall continued to do stunts over their heads
for ten minutes, surpassing all the acrobatics that the
enraged Boches had ever seen even over their own
peaceful aërodromes.

Jimmy exhausted his spirits at about the time the

Huns had exhausted all their available ammunition and we started blithely for home. Swooping down to our field side by side, we made a quick landing and taxied our victorious machines up to the hangars. Then jumping out we ran to each other, extending glad hands for our first exchange of congratulations. And then we noticed that the squadron pilots and mechanics were streaming across the aërodrome towards us from all directions. They had heard the news while we were still dodging shrapnel and were hastening out to welcome our return. The French had telephoned in a confirmation of my first victory, before I had had time to reach home. Not a single bullet hole had punctured any part of my machine.

The months of May and June, 1918, saw the Ninety-fourth Squadron of the First Pursuit Group becoming a veteran organization. The casualties of our men began to mount. The first man killed was Chapman, shot down in flames near Nancy. Then the great American pilot, Lufbery, was killed by a German two-seater in a sensational manner. Hall was lost in a fight on the enemy's side, when the fabric was stripped from one of his wings and a spent three-inch artillery projectile actualy lodged between two of the cylinders of his rotary motor.* He was made a prisoner.

During this period Douglas Campbell of the Ninety-fourth obtained the greatest number of victories and was the first American ace in the group. The First Pursuit Group gained a great deal of experience by sending patrols deep into the enemy's territory and by protecting two-seater airplanes that were carrying out reconnaissances and photographing. One day the commander of the British Independent Air Force, who was bombing the interior cities of Germany, asked me if I would not lend him assistance, as the German pursuit airplanes were shooting down so many of his planes. I immediately assigned the First Pursuit Group to this protection

*This incident is recounted by Charles Nordhoff and James Norman Hall himself in their Knights of the Blue, which appeared last summer in Liberty and came out as a book with the title Falcons of France. They attributed the misadventure to Charles Selden, the imaginary pilot who tells their composite true story.

duty. The next day, as the British bombers returned, a patrol of our airplanes hovered in the sun watching for enemy Albatrosses. Sure enough, they came, and our men shot down several, thereby saving the British bombardment squadron. In this Rickenbacker distinguished himself, leading the flight and again shooting down an adversary.

Other pilots, such as Meissner, Chambers, Buford, Biddle, and Hambleton, distinguished themselves during this period. In June, as German attacks had become so incessant, particularly in the Château-Thierry salient, where the Sixth French Army had been virtually destroyed, it was decided to push in all the American troops available so as to stop the German advance. We knew now that our airmen would be pitted against the flower of the German aviation, the famous Richthofen Flying Circus and other veteran organizations. The only organizations I had available were the First Pursuit Group and three observation squadrons. With these we went to Château-Thierry. Rickenbacker was detailed to bring up the rear of the First Pursuit Group so as to help out any men who lagged behind, who were forced to land or lost their way.

Upon our arrival in the Château-Thierry area, we immediately entered into full combat against the enemy's best organizations and our losses were proportionately high. Here we lost Alan Winslow, who had shot down the first enemy airplane at Toul. Fortunately he escaped with the loss of his left arm. He later became my aide. Quentin Roosevelt was another one lost. We were under French command and were forced to send out small patrols along the front to protect observation airplanes attached to the infantry. The Germans would see these small patrols and concentrate two or three times their number against them and shoot them out of the sky.

This system could only lead to our total destruction. I brought the matter up before the French commanding general and told him that in a flight across the German position at Château-Thierry and Soissons I had found great depots of ammunition and supplies at Fère-en-Tardenois, and that if we could obtain some bombing airplanes to attack the place the Germans would have to defend it and thus their pursuit aviation would be taken off our front. We asked the

French to give us some bombers, but they replied that their aviation was tired out and could spare no ships for that purpose, as they had been in constant combat for the last three months. We asked the British and they responded by sending five squadrons, three bomber and two pursuit.

Immediately we attacked Fère-en-Tardenois from the air, the First Pursuit Group with Rickenbacker participating. Twelve of our airplanes were lost as the Germans desperately defended this, their central supply point for the whole drive along the Marne. Our air bombs blew up several ammunition depots, however, and the enemy suffered the loss of thirty airplanes shot down. Our air force was now acting in a concentrated mass and the enemy, not knowing when to expect us, could keep only about one-third of their airplanes in the air at one time. The tables were turned. We had seized the initiative and were carrying the war into their country.

Rickenbacker, in one of the combats, was driven down by several of the enemy Fokkers from an altitude of 18,000 feet. He had to dive all the way with his full engine and it broke his eardrums, which made him ill and he had to go to the hospital in Paris.

At this time I was able to get new airplanes for the First Pursuit Group. The Nieuport 28, which we had at first, although fast and the most maneuverable plane on the front, was weak structurally. They were subject to breaks in the air and having the fabric come off the wings. They had not been used by the French for that reason, but they were the only thing we could get and they really did very well in our hands. But now we had to have better ones, and I had long before requested that the whole American aviation be equipped with the French Spad. Fortunately the French had produced enough so that we could get them. Our Pursuit Group was now equipped with these same French machines, the fastest and strongest airplanes on the Western Front.

In the latter part of July it was decided that the American army should be concentrated back of St. Mihiel and an attack made first at that point, to throw the Germans out of the salient which stuck into the side of the Allied position, and then we should attack in the Argonne Forest, where no impression had been made on the German position for four years. Our American squadrons were gradually being equipped and sent to the front and I asked that the largest possible number of Allied aircraft be assigned to us for this the first great battle of the American army. The request was complied with, and at St. Mihiel I had the greatest air force ever assembled under one command, consisting of 1,476 airplanes. Rickenbacker rejoined at St. Mihiel from the hospital and immediately assumed his position as flight commander in the Ninety-fourth Squadron. The Germans knew him well by this time and called him "Von Rickenbacker."

The First Pursuit Group was now the most experienced organization in our service and at St. Mihiel the group was used to patrol the immediate front of our troops, to attack the retreating enemy on the ground, and to shoot down enemy balloons. Rickenbacker distinguished himself in this series of operations. Not only did he shoot down more enemy aircraft but also, by attacking retreating German troops on the ground and their automobiles, horse artillery, and motor trucks, he and the group caused the roads to become so piled up and choked with trucks and dead animals that large organizations of Germans surrendered to our infantry rather than be shot to pieces from the air while retreating along those roads.

We were now bombing the enemy at night with our airplanes and pursuing him in the daytime.

On the 24th of September we started the attack in the Argonne Forest. Four thousand two hundred cannon opened the show. The concussion from the fire of these guns was so great that a flight of airplanes stationed at Verdun, about three miles from the front, had their gasoline tanks loosened so they actually leaked.

I had noticed that the Ninety-fourth Squadron was having fewer and fewer airplanes available for duty shown on its morning report and I called Major Harney, the commander of the group, to account for the poor showing. He replied that the squadron commander should be changed and I told him to do it at once and put the most efficient person in command. We picked as commanders for all organizations those who demonstrated in the face of the enemy their ability to lead their men personally in combat and set an example to those around them. Hartney said that Rickenbacker was the man, and he was immediately put in command of the squadron. The next day, from having six or seven airplanes out of twenty-four available for duty, the squadron had eighteen; and so it continued.

When we attacked in the Argonne, the First Pursuit Group was assigned to low-altitude patrols and attacking enemy balloons. The day we opened the battle ten balloons were shot down by this organization. Rickenbacker led his squadron. On the second day I noticed that the transport in the center of our infantry position had become so horribly clogged at a little village in the center of our lines that it could move neither backward nor forward. It was the ideal time for the enemy to counterattack, because neither could the front line have been supplied with ammunition or food nor could reënforcements be sent up along the road.

Immediately the German aviation started to take advantage of this, but not before I had sent the First Pursuit Group to attack them whenever they appeared near the lines or on the enemy side. At this time the First Pursuit Group flew right through the artillery and machine-gun barrages of both sides; also, it was constantly subjected to antiaircraft fire of all kinds. Again our losses were heavy. Rickenbacker was always in the forefront of the attack. During this time, after he had shot down two enemy airplanes in one day, he became our ace of aces, the man with the most victories.

Luke, a remarkable pilot in the First Pursuit Group, had been assigned to the destruction of balloons. He shot down ten enemy aircraft in one week, four in one day, and was then killed himself. No such record as this was ever made in any other service, French, British, or German.

Rickenbacker barely escaped with his life in many of these combats, returning with the holes of the enemy's bullets through his plane. One day I was coming back in my plane from a reconnaissance over the front when suddenly I saw below me a flight of our Spads apparently attacking an enemy airplane away inside our lines. Coming down lower, I noticed a German two-seater airplane below them, and wondered why they did not shoot it down at once. Then I saw the observer in the rear cockpit standing up with his arms folded. He was out of ammunition. It was Rickenbacker's flight that was trying to herd him into our lines and force him down without having to kill the crew. Lower and lower went the German, but they could not make him land. At last they fired a couple of bullets through his gas tank and engine and he came down. Neither the pilot nor the observer was killed and the airplane was not severely damaged, though damaged too much for us to repair and fly it.

All our aircraft were now beginning to fly not only by day but by night, taking off in the dark of early morning and coming back after nightfall. In the middle of October, General Pershing received information that we would be counterattacked heavily by German reënforcements coming from beyond the right of our line. He told me it was imperative to get information about this at once. It was dark and the atmosphere was none too clear.

I called on Colonel Hartney, the commander of the First Pursuit Group, to ask for volunteers to carry out this very dangerous and important mission. The pilots had to fly at low altitude, something like one or two hundred feet, observe everything on the roads and railroads, note the number of lights seen, whether they were fixed or moving, and the position of any objects which they saw on the roads in their vicinity.

Rickenbacker and two others were the first to volunteer and were sent. Fortunately all of them returned with reports which showed conclusively that no such movement of the enemy was taking place. Rickenbacker was nearly lost on this trip, as his compass failed to work, and only by being able to see the North Star did he get back so he could see the searchlight beacon which had been put up as a guide.

Toward the last of October and first of November, Rickenbacker was the leading squadron commander of the American aviation. The squadron consisted of twenty-five airplanes. Our aviation was being rapidly expanded. Had the war lasted until the spring of 1919, we would have had the greatest aviation of any nation on the Western Front. Rickenbacker was just about to be given command of a group of one hundred airplanes when the Armistice was signed, probably saving his life, because ordinarily the life of the leading ace of a service does not last indefinitely. However, had the war continued and had he lived, he undoubtedly would have commanded a brigade of air force in the spring of 1919 and been a general officer.

This account of some of Rickenbacker's work has been written by me to show what intelligent and persistent effort to become a great fighter will do. We had many of them, some of whom might have equaled Rickenbacker's string of victories had the war continued.

These men were a remarkable lot, quick, cool, of the highest type of American manhood. No champions in any war ever fought such hand-to-hand duels, where if they failed the odds against their surviving were so great, as the air fighters of the war in Europe.

It has been a great source of satisfaction to me to see these men who so highly distinguished themselves in their service against the enemy become leaders in the walks of life in which fate has taken them. Rickenbacker has done so. He may at this time be considered one of the captains of industry of the United States.

Air power is the backbone of a country's national defense, and the fighting pilots in the American aviation in the Great War proved to the world that they were second to none.

Leaves from My War Diary

BY GEN. WILLIAM MITCHELL

[*Editor's Note: General "Billy" Mitchell was in command of American air forces during the decisive battles of 1918. His opportunities to observe the war were unsurpassed, and this selection from his diary deals with the major offensives of the war's final phase, up to the Armistice and the occupation of Germany.*

The great German assault was launched on March 21, 1918, destroying the British Fifth Army. In early April the onslaught slackened. The fate of the Allies hung in the balance, and no one knew where Ludendorff, the German general, would aim his next staggering blow.]

◎ ◎ ◎ ◎ ◎ ◎ ◎ ◎ ◎

PART ONE

April, 1918.

The Fifth British Army is a thing of the past and a great gaping hole exists in the line. The British Army is a running mass of fugitives.

General Foch apparently had anticipated an attack and had brought up troops from Italy and had thrown them in yesterday where I saw them. We hear that as a result of these operations General Foch has been made the supreme commander of all the armed forces in northern France. It is high time to have a single directing head; there has been too little coordination in the past.

The British have a single commander for all the navies.

Later on we must have a single commander for all the air forces.

The Germans have hit at the right time, for they know our American troops are not quite ready. But they soon will be. We have several divisions which, if put on the defensive, could give an excellent account of themselves.

The British are in a bad way, and from General Haig down they are publishing orders to the troops to stand their ground and die in their tracks, as their whole existence as a nation depends on it. The Germans are attempting to completely destroy the British Army, use up the French reserves that must be sent there to help them, and later to fall on the French.

I doubt if they can make a complete success of it, on account of their lack of motor transport. They can lay down temporary railroads with great speed, but they lack sufficient motor transportation to keep up with their infantry, and they also need more air power.

The hole in the British Army is twenty or thirty miles broad. Hodges of our Engineering Corps, I have heard, dug a line of trenches for the British to occupy around Amiens, which they are in now and are trying to hold. If the Germans had a few divisions of cavalry with armored motor trucks following them, well supported by tanks and air forces, they could win the war within a month or two; but I am sure they have not sufficient forces of any of these to do it.

On March 28 I looked over the equipment of the First Squadron at Le Bourget. They were getting old airplanes and not the latest models—Spad two-seaters with the Hispano engine, a dangerous outfit for observation work.

I started my flight back to Neufchâteau and looked over the roads running up to the great battle. They were filled everywhere with transport, artillery, and troops moving to the scene of the fray.

I arrived at Neufchâteau without incident, and reported what I had seen to General Liggett, and what my estimate of the situation was. Liggett was itching to get into the fight and thought that four of our divisions could do good work, and I believed they could.

I went down to Chaumont and saw Harbord on March 31. He told me that General Pershing had offered to put any or all of our troops into the line in this great crisis. We now must have half a million men in France. While untrained— many of them have never even fired a rifle—they certainly can do a great deal if given a chance.

It is strange how quickly the French people sense what is going on. Word travels like wildfire through northern France. Although no news is allowed to be published in the papers of what is happening to the British Army, every inhabitant of the Upper Marne knows that the great crisis is at hand. Everybody knows that as soon as the attacks against the British Army subside a little the French Army will be jumped on and thousands of their sons will pay the price of their defense.

Early in April I was occupied with an attempt to get suitable airplanes for our men. It now is apparent that no airplanes made in America can be put on the front before the end of the year. Those in authority in America had not followed our recommendations as to what kind of airplanes we wanted, so that a misfit combination of observation, day bombardment, and pursuit airplane, with a motor that had never been tried, was to be our principal ship to come from the United States. That is, the DH4 airplane with the Liberty engine.

The Germans were beginning to hit Paris with their long-range cannon. This gun was shooting about seventy-two miles. Many people thought at first that the projectiles had been dropped by airplanes, as they did not believe that a gun could be constructed that would shoot so far. A measurement of the curvature of some of the fragments of the projectile told what size the gun was, and from the angle at which the shots fell it could be told about where the gun was located.

Airplanes were immediately sent over to attempt to find it; but because its position was so well concealed, and because of dummy positions constructed near it, it was very difficult for the airplanes to either locate or destroy it.

The object of the Germans in this long-range bombardment was to congest all of the lines of communication, railroads and roads around Paris, just at the time that they were to bring on another offensive against the French Army, thereby making it difficult for the French to move supplies rapidly through this area to their troops.

It was also intended to scare the ammunition workers, government employees, and citizens so that they would evacuate the city to some extent at least.

The Germans were largely successful in this, as there was quite an exodus from Paris. The city was darkened every night, as German airplane raids were made at the same time. Numbers of additional anti-aircraft cannon, with their crews, were withdrawn from the armies and put around the city. These did little good in keeping the German attack off. Many searchlights were placed at appropriate points. Balloon barrages—that is, small balloons holding up wires— were sent up to a height of about five or six thousand feet.

In spite of the terrible mess into which our Air Service had been projected as a result of so many nonflying officers being at the top, some order is beginning to come out of it. Dunwoody is doing excellent work with the supplies in the interior of France. I received a funny note from Dunwoody, which showed about the way things are going on.

Everything is being handled by conferences because no one individual will take the responsibility. The result is that, as the officers composing the conferences know nothing about the subject, the wrong thing is invariably done because the line of least resistance is always followed, no matter whether it is good or bad.

Following is the note that I received from Dunwoody:

AMERICAN EXPEDITIONARY
FORCES
U. S. AIR SERVICE

April 18, 1918.

HULLO:

How is the zone of Advance?

Have just returned from Tours. Is this the thing you wanted? My visit made me think of it.

A Conference is a collection of human beings of almost superhuman intelligence, gathered together for the purpose of passing a series of resolutions based on their combined ignorance of a particular subject.

As a general rule, every Conference faces a crisis.

Every Conference has a main bore, an auxiliary bore, and other bores stationed at strategic points. When anybody ventures an original idea it is the duty of the main bore to head it off. He usually succeeds.

In spite of all these things, we are actually getting squadrons up on the line. The aviation schools in the interior, under Colonel Kilner, are doing excellent work and turning out pilots who, as far as training away from the front is concerned, are by far the best in Europe.

Kilner not only stays around the schools, but he frequently comes up to the front to see what we want and need in training and goes back and applies it. I consider him the most competent commander of aëronautical training schools that we have.

The First Observation Squadron made its first patrol over the line, with Major Royce commanding, on April 11. Our Ninety-fourth Pursuit Squadron moved to Toul on April 8, and the Ninety-first Army Observation Squadron came up. We are forming the nucleus of our bombardment aviation, also. All of these squadrons are now definitely assigned to my command and we are working hard on their battle training.

When we can't get them, the men that have had experience in the French or British service over the lines and in whom the pilots have confidence are put into the key positions.

Among these men is Major Raoul Lufbery, who leads the Americans in the number of enemy airplanes shot down. Lufbery's father is an American citizen; his mother was a French peasant woman.

Lufbery at first was a very poor pilot, but gradually he developed into one of the greatest experts in individual combat that there is on the Western Front. We are very fortunate in having him come up with the first pursuit squadrons that are arriving at Toul.

All eyes are on our men. As far as actual pilotage and flying is concerned, they really are wonderful. Of course, never having been exposed in actual combat, it is a question as to what will happen. Our First Pursuit Squadron on the line, the Ninety-fourth, has adopted a catchy insignia for its ships.

It shows Uncle Sam's hat with a ring around it to signify that Uncle Sam has entered the ring of the European War to take up active fighting on his part. [NOTE: Major John Huffer, in command of the squadron, and almost every pilot in it later became famous for feats of arms over the front.]

We, of course, are still under French command; but I arranged with the commander of French Aviation of the Eighth French Army to give us a definite sector to defend, and we were given the area between the Meuse and the Moselle rivers. That is, our left is at St. Mihiel and our right at Pont-à-Mousson. This is the first definite sector assigned to an American flying organization.

A bit of rare good fortune happened to us on our very first day of independent operations on the front. I believe that what occurred was the most important thing that ever happened to American fighting aviation. It gave our men a confidence that could have been obtained in no other way.

It must be remembered that we are entering the war with our fliers to fight men who have been at it for three years and are as great fliers as the world has ever seen. They have splendid airplanes, splendid machine guns, are excellently instructed, and have a fine organization behind them.

The eventful day was April 14. We had sent a patrol out early in the morning, consisting of Captain Peterson, Lieutenant Rickenbacker, and Lieutenant Chambers, with orders to go up to 5,000 meters and intercept any enemy airplanes that crossed the line. I wanted to stop all German photographic machines that were taking pictures of our back areas where our troops were being assembled.

Lieutenants Campbell, Winslow, and Meisner were ordered to stand by on the alert at the airdrome, ready to take the air at a moment's notice.

The morning of the 14th dawned rather cold and foggy; but our patrol proceeded over the front, where it was discovered by the German lookouts and anti-aircraft artillery posts. Our patrol became separated in the fog, but fortunately returned to the field at Toul without mishap.

Shortly after the return of this patrol, the anti-aircraft artillery station on the top of Mont St. Michel, just outside of Toul, signaled that some German airplanes were approaching the city above the fog; and our alert, consisting of Campbell, Winslow, and Meisner, was ordered to take the air.

The whir of the German motors could be heard by the citizens of Toul, and also the roar of the American engines at the same time as they took off. Meisner could not start his ship, and therefore remained on the ground.

Hundreds in the city and vicinity of Toul looked to see what would happen. A remarkable picture met their gaze. The German machines, concealed by the fog, had not yet put in appearance; but just as the two American ships approached the cloud ceiling, the German planes came out of it, and were instantly attacked by Allan Winslow and Douglas Campbell.

Winslow shot the first plane down, and Campbell the

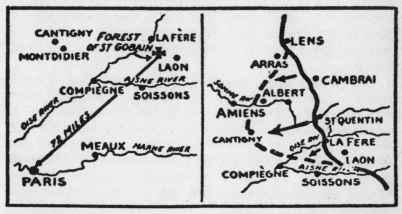

Map showing location of the forest of St. Gobain from which the German long-range gun (X) shelled Paris, seventy-two miles away.

Where the German armies broke through the British lines in Ludendorff's terrific drive of March, 1918.

second. Both German airplanes had been brought down, and our pilots were back on the airdrome within four and one-half minutes after they left it. It was the most remarkable exhibition ever given on the Western Front, and in full view of all the soldiers and citizens residing in that part of the country.

Neither of the German pilots was killed. One of them was a very capable officer, the other also a good man. They reported that they had been ordered to attack two enemy machines that were crossing the lines between St. Mihiel and Pont-à-Mousson. That undoubtedly was the patrol consisting of Rickenbacker and Chambers that had become lost in the fog.

I have always thought that another thing was intended. The Germans knew full well that our air units had just reached the line. In all probability our men, new at the game, might not be as alert or as competent in their work as they would be at a later date. Some German machines near this area had recently come right down on to the French airdrome at Toul, set fire with their flaming bullets to some French airplanes on the ground, and had shot up the whole place, killing several people.

If they could do this to the Americans right off the handle, it would have a dampening effect on our morale and would greatly increase that of the German Aviation. I have always thought that, taking advantage of the fog on that day, these German airplanes were attempting to do that very thing.

The remains of the enemy airplanes were taken into the square at Toul by order of the French commanding officer and the mayor of the city. The enthusiasm of the citizens was tremendous. I lost no time in publishing these facts all over the Army and to our Aviation in particular. I brought General Liggett to pay a visit to the squadron a day or so after; and he, with his usual affability, congratulated the officers and definitely showed his appreciation for what they had done.

We now are in full action on the front, and each day our men show up to better and better advantage—Rickenbacker, Chambers, Meisner, and many others. We have our losses too, which I shall not mention in this chronicle.

The burning of a pilot in the air, as his ship catches fire from the hostile flaming bullets, is a terrible thing. When wounded, he falls, and thousands of feet instead of two or three, as a man on the ground does. We are inflicting a loss of at least three to one on the enemy, which is absolutely remarkable for a new outfit. Our men are full of dash, well instructed, and exceptionally cool in combat.

Some amusing things have happened. One of our hospital

units, with a number of good-looking nurses, moved into a French hospital only about a mile away from the airdrome of the First Pursuit Group. Our pilots were delighted and overjoyed to meet these nice American girls; and each evening, when they could get off or sneak off, they went over to the hospital to see them.

The commanding officer of the hospital, one of our regular surgeons and an old friend of mine, came over to see me one day, and told me that the work of his hospital being very much interfered with by our young men. He said he had no objections to their coming to see the nurses; but they stayed up so late at night that the nurses were good for nothing the next day and he wished that I would tell the pilots to bring them back earlier.

Accordingly, I sent word out that there was no objection to our officers going to the hospital when they could, but that the work of the hospital was being interefered with, and that when our young men went to see the nurses they must get them back there at an early hour.

I heard nothing more about this for some days, when the commanding officer of the hospital came in to see me again. This time he seemed quite put out. He told me that, although most of our pilots had complied with the order that I had sent, some of them had not, and that he had found it necessary to issue orders to the nurses that none of them should go out or see our pilots. The order had been issued the day before.

That morning, he reported, several of our airplanes in formation had flown over the hospital and had bombarded it with long rolls of tissue paper, which was then covering the tops of the building and hanging up in the telephone and telegraph wires. This performance greatly interfered with the discipline of his whole organization and he wished some drastic action to be taken.

I went out to the hospital with him to see what had happened. It presented an amusing sight. The paper had been dropped in rolls and unraveled on the way down, and was all over everything. It was the most amusing thing I had ever seen. Of course I knew who did it, but took no action beyond telling them to cut out all foolishness in the future, which they did.

The thing that I most greatly lack is superior commanders for our larger air units. There are practically no officers of the regular Army that are competent. None of them have had experience in war, and, with very few exceptions, none of them are good enough pilots.

On the other hand, there are many temporary officers; that is, those who have come in during the war, who are perfectly capable of handling organizations of any size. With these men the power of initiative and quick perception, the ability to assume responsibility and to act at once on their convictions is away ahead of that possessed by the regular officers.

There are some exceptions to this. Colonel T. D. Milling of the regular Army, one of our oldest pilots, has constantly attempted to get a command on the front. Royce has done well. And Brereton, who has just come up with the Twelfth Observation squadron, appears to be a good man.

The nonflying aggregation, who are all-powerful in aviation, attempt to put nonfliers into the upper positions so as to get the rank. How many of our pilots are killed as a result of this seems to be a secondary consideration with them.

Another kaleidoscopic change has taken place in our air organization; and General Foulois has his headquarters in Tours, but spends most of the time in Paris, where Dunwoody is really doing good work. There is no Air Service liaison officer at Chaumont.

The General Staff is now trying to run the Air Service with just as much knowledge of it as a hog knows about skating. It is terrible to have to fight with an organization of this kind, instead of devoting all our attention to the powerful enemy on our front.

I have had many talks with General Pershing on this subject, some of them very heated, with much pounding on the table on both sides. One time he told me that if I did not stop insisting that the organization of the Air Service be changed he would send me home. I answered that if he did he would soon come after me. This made him laugh and our talk ended amicably.

He did not know how badly the Air Service was off, because he did not know enough about it. Furthermore, he had to be cautious with a new arm such as this, and he made haste slowly.

One evening I went over to Nancy in the French sector for dinner, and when we were about halfway there I noticed that the moon was shining and figured that it would not be long before the German bombers were around. I had my car ready at the door to leave quickly in case the alarm sounded.

No lights appeared in the city, but from the air, with a bright moon, it certainly must have been as plain as day. Suddenly the alarm was sounded, and I got in my automobile and drove rapidly for the hill in the vicinity of Pont

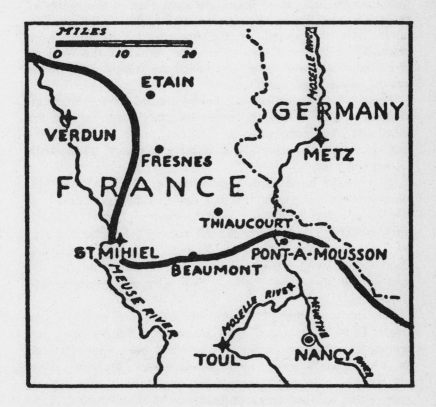

Lieutenant A. F. Winslow (at left), who shot down a plane on the first day the American Air Service operated independently at the front. The map shows the first sector assigned to the United States Air Force, the heavy line indicating the German front.

St. Vincent. As we approached it we could hear the engines of the German airplanes.

I wanted to get up the hill, so that from this point of vantage I could look down and see exactly what happened. The anti-aircraft fire was incessant, and the searchlights swept backward and forward over the sky, finding nothing, as usual. Suddenly I heard three loud reports, one after the other, and saw the great flashes on the ground as if from some great shell exploding. Then everything was quiet.

Still the buzz of the German airplanes kept up, so I continued to watch. Suddenly there were three more explosions, and after the last one a great fire sprang up in the center of the town and apparently spread to various buildings. We could hear the sound of the fire engines as they went through the streets to the scene. The sound of the German airplanes died away, and I returned to Nancy and looked around to see what had happened.

The first three shots had been directed at an ammunition factory. One had hit across the street from it, and the other two had gone straight through the roof and entirely destroyed the factory. It will never make any more shells during this war.

The second three shots were directed at the railroad station. One of them went through the roof of the station and did a good deal of damage which, however, can be repaired very quickly. The second one fell among the railroad tracks and just blew out a big hole. The third one hit a railroad train loaded with gasoline and set it on fire, and the fire had spread to several houses. Two German airplanes had done this.

Just think of what 200 would do if they had them to send over! That is, provided they wanted to destroy the city, which I doubt very much. Nancy has been evacuated almost completely by its civil population on account of the air attacks. Not many troops are quartered in the city. If they were, the Germans undoubtedly would bomb it to a greater extent.

About a month ago, Harbord and De Chambrun had an experience with bombs in Nancy, which gave Harbord a very good insight into what airplanes can do. I think Harbord had the idea, as most ground officers have, that bombs were not particularly effective.

In this instance he had gone to Nancy to have dinner and spend the night. He was in his room in the hotel when the alarm sounded, and, instead of getting at once into the cave under the hotel for protection, he foolishly stayed in his room in the third story.

A bomb hit in the street directly opposite his room and demolished the whole side of the hotel, and, I believe, blew him into the bathtub, with a window casing around his neck for a necklace. If a few more of our General Staff officers could have this same experience, without hurting them any more than it did Harbord, it would be an excellent thing.

I also, out of bravado, stayed aboveground in my first airplane raid a year ago, and learned not to do it if I wanted to stay among the living. An experience like that also shows that if we get sufficient bombardment aviation we can bring the war to a close by carrying it to the vital points in the interior of Germany and making the people sue for peace.

The relation of our aviation with the French is very cordial on both sides. Our pilots appreciate the French pilots and the French pilots appreciate ours.

In the area behind us the British are building up an independent air force. It is the first force of this kind that has ever been gotten together. It is designed to attack the interior cities of Germany.

The British have now combined all their air power under a separate ministry, which is coequal with the Army and Navy. This is a very sensible organization, and one that we should have.

Our Navy is trying to have an air service now, the way the British Navy did at the beginning of the war. They haven't any airplanes to supply their men, but have many pilots. I now have some French airplanes, but not enough pilots. The Navy is going to conduct an air war of their own somewhere—nobody knows where exactly.

This performance just means a tremendous waste of money, men, and energy. All of our aëronautical resources should be put here with my organization and fought as one great American unit that can give a combined punch where needed.

I continue to fly over the lines almost every day and keep track of each organization, each commanding officer, and almost each pilot. How much more fun it would be to be a pilot in one of the squadrons.

I remember in the Spanish War, when I was a private in the First Wisconsin Infantry, I had more fun than at any other time, and wanted to stay one. My father, however, who was then in the United States Senate, made me accept a discharge and later a commission, which, of course, was a good thing, but was not as pleasant as being with my old comrades from our home town in our local company.

Our First Observation Squadron is now acting with our Twenty-sixth Division under General Edwards. This is the first time that our own air forces have definitely acted with our own troops.

It was apparent to me that we ought to have an American rest station for our aviators as close as practicable to the line. A few days' rest in peace and quiet often saves a good man who would be permanently incapacitated if kept at it longer.

The Countess de Fénelon had offered her beautiful château at Cirey for this purpose, so I had it regularly taken over by the Red Cross.

Mr. Osborne of the Red Cross made the arrangements. He is a fine fellow, one of the tallest men I have ever seen—he must measure six feet seven or eight inches. He is handling the Red Cross operations at Neufchâteau in a very efficient manner.

The Germans continue to hit the British Army. Their object is either to destroy it or to take all the fight out of it, so that the British can do nothing for the rest of the summer. Just now the British are fighting desperately, with their backs to the wall. There is no talk of hitting back, but only of whether they will be able to hold out or not. It is a very serious situation.

PART TWO

May, 1918.

WE now have an actual observation group acting with two squadrons in it, the First and the Twelfth. We have a pursuit group composed of the Ninety-fourth, Ninety-fifth, Twenty-seventh, and 194th squadrons, with an air park, under command of Major Atkinson. We have an army observation squadron, the Ninety-first, and a bombardment squadron is almost ready to come up to the front. From now on our force will grow rapidly.

We are now not only using our squadrons on the front, but we are having maneuvers and aërial instruction with the

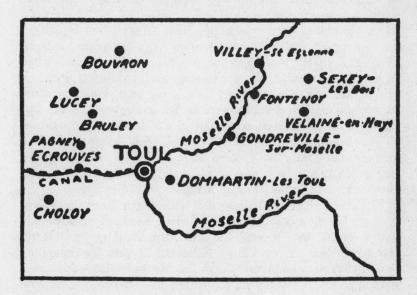

A map showing Toul and the vicinity where the battle took place in which Lufbery, America's famous ace, was killed.

ground troops at the schools and in the training areas. Our infantry divisions are beginning to come up, one after another. We have all the equipment that money can buy—that is, experience and a good corps of officers.

Both of these will come with work on the front, but will be purchased at a tremendous cost in lives. What we need at home is a good nucleus of citizen soldiers. The idea of intrusting everything to a small regular army, which in truth is not an army, but merely a national constabulary organized for peacetime duty, is poor national economy.

Brereton has taken the Twelfth Squadron over to the Baccarat sector, and I went over to see him. A British two-seater DH airplane attempted to dive on a German ship in that vicinity. Both wings had come off the British plane, and the fuselage, like a projectile, had shot to the ground with its living freight.

Another British airplane landed with bombs where our Ninety-sixth Bombardment Squadron is stationed. In taking off, the pilot stalled the machine, which fell to the ground and caught fire. The bombs exploded immediately. A piece of the fur collar of the pilot or the observer was found afterward, and also the heel of a shoe.

The airplanes with which the First Observation Squadron are equipped are Spad two-seaters with Hispano engines. They are utterly worthless for observation work, and when heavily loaded with their cameras and machine guns are very dangerous. We have lost some good men, killed uselessly as a result of being equipped with these airplanes. I am trying hard to get Salmsons for all our observation squadrons.

The headquarters of the French Eighth Army desired to present the Croix de Guerre to our officers who had distinguished themselves, and accordingly, on May 15, a formation took place at the Toul airdrome.

There were French troops, and also troops from the Twenty-sixth Division, accompanied by their bands. The ceremony was attended by General Passaga, commanding the Thirty-second French Army Corps, General Liggett, commanding the First American Army Corps, and General Edwards, commanding the Twenty-sixth American Division. General Gérard, commanding the Eighth French Army, and I made the presentations.

We had lost two good men who were on the list for citations: Charles W. Chapman, killed in action, and James Norman Hall, whom we thought at that time was dead. They received the decorations posthumously. Peterson, Rickenbacker, and Meisner were decorated.

Our men continue to do well both in pursuit and observation aviation. As the end of the month approached I felt that we could render a good account of ourselves anywhere that we might be put. Comparatively speaking, we are away ahead of the troops on the ground. If we could only get a sufficient number of good airplanes we could certainly have a terrific fighting aviation within a few months.

The end of May proved to be a very sad period for me. To begin with, Major Lufbery was killed on May 19. Lufbery was our leading pilot, and was a great source of strength on account of the confidence our men had in him and on account of his great ability to impart details of air fighting to them.

I was sitting in my office in Toul on May 19 when the alarm was sounded that a German airplane was near. I looked out of the window and saw the anti-aircraft artillery filling the air with projectiles. The German airplane, a two-seater Albatros, was so close to the ground that I thought it was going to land; but suddenly it arose again.

I dashed for my automobile to get to the Toul airdrome, telling Hall, my operations officer, to notify the French Aviation at Nancy that a German airplane was headed in their direction.

As I left in my automobile I could see one of our airplanes engage the German ship, but in an utterly futile way. The pilot did not close up, but expended all his ammunition uselessly in the air. For this performance I have sent the pilot to the rear.

I hurried for the airdrome, but was stopped by a foolish sentinel on the way in who asked me where my pass was. As I arrived on the field I saw an airplane cutting across to head off the German ship. This I was told was Lufbery.

As we had had several patrols out over the front that morning, there was nobody else ready to go after the German machine at that time. As it was too late for me to get in the air, I returned to the office and went to work.

Within a few minutes my telephone rang, and I was informed that Major Lufbery had been killed. His plane had fallen at a little place about six miles from Toul on the Moselle River. A detail from the First Pursuit Group under the commanding officer had gone over there to get the remains, so I ran over to find out what I could about his last fight.

The little village is on a high bank which gradually slopes off to the Moselle. At this time of the year it is covered with flowers and fruit trees in bloom. Lufbery's body had fallen out of his plane into the back yard of an old shoemaker's house. The shoemaker's daughter, a girl of about sixteen years, lived with him.

Their back yard is a typical French back yard of that class of people. There are little boxes for rabbits, a place for a cow and chickens. A long white picket fence separates the yard from others. Along the fence on both sides there is a fringe of flowers. It was on this picket fence that Lufbery had fallen. One of the pickets pierced his left leg and unquestionably greatly broke the fall. He hit the ground and lay on his back, dead.

The shoemaker's daughter rushed to Lufbery's body and, opening his flying suit, saw his decorations and recognized him immediately. Lufbery was a great hero among the French peasants, because his mother was a peasant. The girl immediately covered the body with flowers and waited for others to come and carry it to the town hall, where our men received it.

The old shoemaker's description of the combat was the best that anybody gave me. He said that all of a sudden the alarm of the approach of a German airplane was sounded.

The people ran for the cellars. But immediately afterward the roar of an American airplane could be heard, and the people yelled to each other: "The Americans are coming—we will be saved." Many then came out of their cellars.

The large German plane was close to the ground, and the pilot and observer could be plainly seen. At the same time, coming from the direction of Toul with an unbelievable speed, a single small American airplane approached the German.

He came straight up on to the tail, and it looked as if the

two airplanes touched each other. Four or five shots were
fired by the American, but the German did not reply. The
American turned quickly, climbed in the air, and came
straight for the German, again under his tail. Again the airplanes looked as if they were touching; again shots were fired
by the American. The German replied with only four or five.

The American airplane drew off gradually, turned upside
down, and it looked as if a sack filled with something fell
out of it. It was the pilot, Lufbery.

Smoke then began coming out of the plane. It caught fire
and glided several hundred yards, when it crashed and
burned up. There was no mark on Lufbery's body except one
bullet shot through the left hand.

It appeared very probable that either his controls were cut,
causing the airplane to turn over, and he fell out, or that he
jumped out because it was on fire. I doubt very much if an
old pilot like Lufbery would have jumped on account of fire.
All the eyewitnesses I talked to said Lufbery fell out before
the plane caught fire.

I think it quite probable that Lufbery, in his hurry to get
after the German plane, failed to tie himself in the plane
with his belt; that the German shots cut his controls, his airplane turned over, and Lufbery fell out. Just think—if he had
had a parachute he could easily have been saved!

Lufbery had never shot an airplane down on our side of
the line. All his combats had been in enemy territory. And he
was terribly anxious to shoot one down where we could get
at the wreck, both on his own account and to show our new
pilots how it was done.

The German airplane proceeded on its way. It was attacked by some pilots from the French Pursuit Group at
Malzéville under Captain de Rode. The German machine
was forced to land and the pilot and observer were captured.

The action of this German crew was remarkable. They had
been sent over to distract attention from another airplane
that was flying at a high altitude for the purpose of taking
photographs.

The Germans at first sent over several airplanes at high
altitude. Our men shot them down. They were followed by
pairs of airplanes. Again our men shot them down. Our

Nieuports were now able to go as high as the German Rumplers. Finding that this scheme did not work, the Germans sent over an airplane at high altitude and one at low altitude, knowing full well that the one at low altitude would probably not return.

The bravery and devotion of this German crew can be imagined; although they had killed one of the best men, either in the French service or in ours, they were held in great respect for their daring fight. There is more chivalry left among our airmen than is the case with the ground troops.

In this war the ground troops seldom meet their adversary face to face. They are operating out of dirty wet ditches, covered by dust, smoke, mud, and fragments of shells and machine-gun bullets or by gas clouds. All this talk about closing up with the bayonet is largely a myth. When troops get close enough for that, one side or the other breaks and runs away. War on the ground nowadays resolves itself into an attack of masses that employ missile-throwing weapons to keep the adversary as far off as possible.

In the air the action is entirely individual as far as combat is concerned. Each man singles out his adversary and they engage in mortal combat. Already we have received notes from the Germans, dropped on our airdromes, as to what has become of the pilots we have lost, and with a request for information as to their pilots whom we have shot down.

On May 20 we buried Lufbery in a little cemetery beyond the Sebastapol Hospital, in the corner of a wood. Already several of our airmen were in it, some killed by the enemy and some killed by the poor machines that we have had to equip our men with. We all assembled and went out to the cemetery with Lufbery's casket piled high with flowers.

General Gérard, General Edwards, and I made short addresses, and while we were doing so the airplanes of our First Pursuit Group flew over, led by Rickenbacker. They came low down and dropped flowers over the grave as the casket was lowered.

The commander of the Independent British Air Force came over and asked me if we could help him in his bombardment raids. He is bombing the area north of Metz with DH4 airplanes in the daytime. He said that when his planes crossed the line the Germans would note the direction of his flight and from that could tell what place he was going to attack.

They would then send pursuit aviation up, wait for the bombardment ships to turn for home, and then attack. The British have lost a good many airplanes with their crews in this way. They have no pursuit aviation with which to protect their bombers. I promised him that we would assist at once.

The next raid that he made, we sent out a patrol to meet the British bombers on the way back. Our patrol maneuvered into the sun, and, sure enough, the German pursuit attacked the British bombers as they neared the line. Our men attacked and dispersed them at once, shooting down three German ships without loss to ourselves. The British are elated over this protection that we have given them.

The hard work and the losses that our men were sustaining without much relaxation were beginning to tell on them a little. As I heard that Miss Elsie Janis, the actress, was to be in our area, I sent over to see if she could come and give an entertainment for our First Pursuit Group. Although she had given three performances that day, she came to the Toul airdrome.

We assembled the pilots, both from the pursuit group and our observation aviation. The men fixed up a stage of boards, held up by gasoline trucks, in an old prewar hangar that was on the flying field. All the windows were shaded so that the lights could not be seen outside and draw fire from a German bomber. The hangar was lighted by electricity generated by one of our machine-shop trucks. Miss Janis gave a remarkable performance which was thoroughly appreciated by our men.

I was having lunch on May 27 at the Café Bosquet in Toul when my adjutant, Captain Kelleher, came to me with a very perturbed look on his face. I could see, as he approached me, there was something serious.

He called me to one side and said: "I have some bad news for you. Your brother has crashed in an airplane." I asked him if he were dead and he said that he was. The accident had occurred at our air depot at Colombey-les-Belles.

He had flown down to Chaumont in the morning to attend to some matters of equipment for the air troops. He had had one forced landing on the way down, due to oil trouble in his engine, but had landed, repaired it, and proceeded on his journey. Coming back, he had attempted to land at Colombey-les-Belles. The airdrome at this place is quite bad.

As he came in to land he had a great deal of speed. His front wheels hit hard and he bounced. He lowered the tail of his ship. The next time the wheels and the tail skid hit hard, and again he bounced. Apparently he decided to make another turn of the field, so he put on his motor and started to make a circle.

When he started to make the turn, the longerons or beams in the back part of the fuselage broke, and the ship fell to earth, and he was instantly killed. It was a weak ship.

Thus died my only brother, a splendid young man of twenty-three years of age. He had everything in him that a brother should have. He was greatly thought of and respected by everyone with whom he came in contact. Major Frank Page took charge of the body and all the arrangements for the funeral, which we held next day in a manner similar to Lufbery's.

This was his first campaign, and it seemed to me that if either of us had to be killed I should have been the one, because I have been in several campaigns before. While primarily his death was due to a weak airplane, I think that his eyes were not as good as they should have been, and that he stretched matters in his physical examination to get by the doctors, in his anxiety to be in the Air Service and be near me.

I have made up my mind more than ever to rely on the judgment of the doctors as to a man's fitness for flight. Our doctors prove their value more and more every day. I have also determined to continue to try every kind of airplane myself, that our men have to use, before adopting it for our service.

Of course, hindsight is better than foresight, but if our government and our army had followed the recommendations that I had made in April, 1917, more than a year ago, which are a matter of record, we would have had good airplanes long before this. But there is no use crying over spilt milk; in a war the only way we can make up for our losses is to fight the enemy more strongly.

It is a tradition in our family that every male that is able goes to war immediately on the outbreak of hostilities. My mother has both her sons and four sons-in-law in the services. She has contributed every male member that she could. She is getting old now, and I am afraid that my brother's death will have a very bad effect on her, although she will never complain or say anything about it.

The death of Lufbery and my brother has been a great spur to the pilots in the First Pursuit Group. They immediately began to put forward redoubled efforts to shoot down the Germans. On the afternoon of my brother's funeral, I got in my airplane and inspected all of the aviation that we had on the front, including the work of the pilots over the line. It certainly is a source of great satisfaction to see how they are perfecting themselves in the short time that they have been on the front.

Douglas Campbell was a great friend of my brother's. He made up his mind to shoot down several German airplanes to make up for John's loss. Campbell and my brother had been among the first ten flying cadets to come to Europe in August, 1917, and were close friends. On the last day of May, Campbell shot down a two-seater in single combat, which crashed just north of the headquarters of our First Division at Ménil-la-Tour.

In this combat the German observer exhausted all his ammunition. Campbell considered letting him go, but on second thought he knew the German aviator had secured valuable photographs of our area, and he shot him down.

The pilot and observer were both officers of the Prussian Army and were given a suitable military burial. Campbell reported that, as he approached for the last shot, the German observer stood in the back seat with his arms folded, looking him squarely in the face. His empty cartridge belt was dangling over the side of the airplane from his machine gun. He was waiting bravely for the death which he knew was sure to come.

Another kaleidoscopic change has taken place in the Air Service. General Mason Patrick, an engineer officer, has been made Chief of the Air Service. General Patrick has always been an efficient engineer officer, and recently has been in charge of what we call utilities in the service of supply.

Things have gotten in such a mess in the interior, however,

that it is necessary to put somebody in charge of things there
that General Pershing has confidence in.

Patrick was in Pershing's class at the Military Academy at
West Point, and has always done good work. He will get
along pretty well if he keeps his hands off the air units that
are actually fighting. If not, he will get into trouble, because
the time has arrived when we are actually fighting hard
against the Germans, and interference by nonfliers will be
disastrous.

Our First Army Corps, under General Liggett, is to be
put into the line as an organization just as soon as it is possible. All the active air units on the front are to be assigned
to it, and I am to retain command of them. General Foulois
is to be assigned as Chief of the Air Service of the First
Army.

Milling is coming up to the front to take command of a
wing. Every two or three months we change the title of our
office, but fortunately we are left fighting the enemy all the

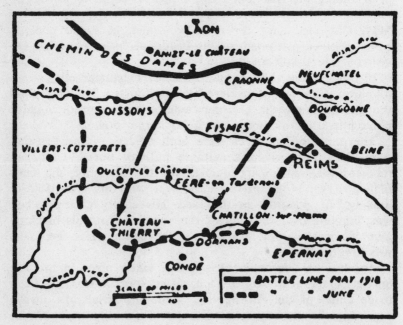

*The German thrust from the Chemin des Dames to the
Marne, just before the A. E. F. helped to stem the advance.*

time. The only actual change that takes place is to get a new rubber stamp out with which to mark the correspondence. I have a good working staff now, and the air units that we have on the line can be rapidly expanded as our men come up.

The English are badly smashed up and are trying to replace their losses in men and equipment. In the meantime they are putting up what amounts to almost a last stand, as is shown by the order issued by General Haig, commanding the British Army, which is as follows:

> Every position must be held to the last man. There must be no retirement. With our backs to the wall, and believing in the justice of our cause, each one of us must fight to the end. The safety of our homes and the freedom of mankind depend alike upon the conduct of each one of us at this critical moment.

The French know that they are to be attacked next, and that the British will be unable to render much help for a while.

June, 1918.

The Germans have attacked the French Army in force. The blow came along the Chemin des Dames, the place where the French thought it might come last autumn, which led to the battle of Malmaison in which the French captured the heights that covered that area.

The Germans used very much the same strategy and tactics against the French in this area as they did against the Fifth British Army in March. The German advance toward the Marne was so fast that the French Army units that stood in their path were entirely destroyed, and even the French airdromes were taken, with the airplanes in them—some 200 planes being lost in this way by the French.

Again there is a tremendous hole in the line and the Germans are advancing rapidly on the Marne. General Foch is being criticized a good deal for not having had more troops where the Germans broke through; but if he put all his troops on the line he would have no mass of maneuver with which to hit a movement by the Germans.

Most of his reserves have been used up in helping the British, though. My friend Major Armengaud, who now is on General Foch's staff, tells me that Foch is trying to get a mass of maneuver together, but at the present time the British are powerless to detach any troops, let alone hold their own. Their army is in terrible shape since the drubbing it got from the Germans, and it will take a couple of months to get on its feet again.

The French have used up their troops that they brought up from Italy to stop the German attack against the English.

The only real reserves are our new American divisions; and these, I understand, General Foch has ordered to the vicinity of Château-Thierry to try to stop the German advances.

Of course, what the Germans are now trying to do is to seize the line of the Marne and occupy the mountain of Reims, which is the key point in that area.

If the Germans are successful in this they will be able to bring up their troops and supplies behind the curtain of the Marne. The mountain of Reims will form a great bridgehead and base of operations for an advance into the heart of France. This point not only has great defensive strength, but it is a splendid point from which to take the offensive, because good roads radiate out from it in all directions.

The Germans are unquestionably attempting to end the war now by one great final campaign. They have taken the punch out of the British by the campaign this spring. We are not yet ready as an army, so that the French must stand the full force of the German blow.

If the Germans do not end the war now, we certainly shall have an army of 1,000,000 men this year and 2,000,000 men next year, and they know it. I doubt if they can get very far, because they are not strong enough in the air, their cavalry is used up, and their automobile transport and armored cars have no rubber tires. They also are very weak in tanks.

Our Second Division is already fighting near Château-Thierry and has helped to stop the German crossing of the Marne.

General Liggett is preparing to move the headquarters of the First Army Corps to Château-Thierry.

The French are terribly afraid of this great German stroke. It is reported that the Germans have shut down all their munition factories because they have enough ammunition to last them until the end of the war, no matter if it takes two or three years. They have taken all the available men from the factories and from the interior of Germany and put them in the ranks for this great attack.

German troops have been brought up from Italy, and reserves and second-line troops from the Russian frontier. Now is the time for us to get into it, whether we are ready or not.

Up to the middle of the month we worked out the manner in which we should take our air forces to the Château-Thierry area. We decided to form them into a brigade under my command. Colonel Milling is to have direct command of a wing at Toul to which all the squadrons coming up from the interior are to be assigned for battle training.

As soon as this was decided, I immediately went to Château-Thierry to the headquarters of the commander of the Third French Army, General Degoutte, to whom I reported. He instructed me to coordinate our work with his Chief of Air Service, Major Gérard.

I have never seen a more stunned group of people than were the officers at the headquarters of the Third French Army, and, for that matter, the troops also.

The French are not at all excitable in the face of danger; in fact, they are probably the coolest of people under that condition. The French troops of the Third Army were away beyond that. They acted as if they had been hit hard in the head with baseball bats.

They had been under a constant attack for nearly a month; they had lost miles of territory, thousands of men, and hundreds of airplanes. There were no reserves to give them. They just had to hold the ground or die. The flower of German Aviation is concentrated over their victorious army. The French Air Division, from its constant duty on the front, is having to recuperate and re-equip.

I immediately selected the points where our various squadrons should go, selected the supply points, and where we would get our gasoline, ammunition, and rations. Colonel Dunwoody in Paris is a great help. It is the first time that we really begin to feel that somebody is behind us in the interior who can get the stuff up.

I organized the movement of our air units from Toul to the Château-Thierry district into three echelons. I sent a part from each group ahead to the airdrome to which the planes were to fly to prepare for their coming. The airplanes then flew directly to their destinations, where they found arrangements already made for them and most of their mechanical personnel on the ground.

The third echelon, called the rear party, remained at the old airdrome, picked up everything that was left, cranked up the machines when they departed, and then caught up to them in their motor trucks.

This was the first movement of our Air Service from one part of the front to another. It was accomplished most successfully. The First Pursuit Group flew as a unit with some seventy planes, and arrived with only two ships absent. These had landed on account of motor trouble, but rejoined the next day.

Our observation squadrons did equally well, and, although equipped with inferior airplanes, still they rendered an excellent account of themselves.

Belleau Wood, an important position near Château-Thierry, had been held by the Second Division for almost a month. On the first of July they were ordered to attack the village of Vaux. The Twelfth Observation Squadron adjusted the fire of the artillery, protected by the First Pursuit Group. Major Brereton piloted the plane—with Lieutenant Hazlett as observer—that started the fight.

Due to their excellent observation work, the city of Vaux was taken, with 500 prisoners, and completely destroyed by the artillery.

We are now engaged in daily and constant fighting. Major Gérard desired that we put patrols along the front, to act defensively against the German observation planes that were coming over to reconnoiter.

This I considered poor strategy, and told him so; but we put it into effect.

Of course, the Germans merely waited until they saw our small patrols of five or six airplanes and then jumped on them with vastly superior numbers.

The best groups of the German Aviation are in front of us. Jagdstaffel One, the famous red-nosed pursuit group formerly commanded by Baron von Richthofen, is against us. Jagdstaffel Two, equally as good, occupies the airdrome at Coincy. Jagdstaffel Three operates from airdromes in the vicinity of St. Quentin.

The commander of each one of these groups has from twenty-five to fifty Allied machines to his credit.

The pilots composing the flights are the most expert the Germans have on the Western Front. The Germans employed formations of from twenty to thirty machines and it was merely suicide for us to continue to act as we did in small patrols.

In a few days we lost Quentin Roosevelt and many other good men.

PART THREE

June, 1918 (continued).

EACH day I took my airplane and flew it along the front. I now had the fastest airplanes on the Western Front assigned to me. I went alone and without protection, because if I took several planes with me we would be slowed up, easily noticed, and certainly brought to combat. This would have interfered with what I was doing as commander of the air forces; that is, watching everything and preparing ahead of time for what we should do.

My only fear was a surprise attack from the direction of the sun, principally. I had become very expert at seeing enemy planes—and our own, for that matter.

As soon as I could, I demanded from Paris that our observation units be furnished complete with Salmson airplanes, the same ones I had asked for a year before. Our poor fellows had been flying the old ARs, Sopwith 1½-strutters, two-seater Spads, and things of that kind which the French discarded long ago and which are completely outclassed by the German machines. They are more or less death traps.

Our pursuit group still has the Nieuport No. 28 airplanes, but these are wearing out and we can get no replacements for them. The German Aviation has been completely equipped with the Fokker D7 airplane, probably the best pursuit ship on the front. This is slightly better than our Nieuport No. 28.

I insisted that we get 220-horsepower Spads for this group at once. I was answered by the usual talk of the nonfliers that our mechanics were not used to fixed motors and only understood the rotary motor in the Nieuports. I answered that our mechanics could handle anything and I was the judge of what airplanes we wanted.

They had a lot of British Sopwith Camel planes with Clerget engines on hand in the interior. They wanted us to take them. This ship I was not familiar with, so I jumped in my plane and flew to our air reserve depot at Orly to try one. A very heavy wind was blowing and the ceiling was low.

I told the commanding officer, Colonel Baldwin, to get me out some Camels as quickly as possible. I was informed that these were very tricky machines—that the day before one of the best pilots had been killed in one. I told them that had nothing to do with what I was there for and that I wanted the airplanes to try at once.

I got into one, taxied down the field, turned it into the wind, and took off. I had risen only a few feet from the ground when the engine absolutely stopped; but I felt it ahead of time, poked the ship's nose down quickly, and landed between two hangars without breaking a wire.

I had choked the Clerget engine by giving it too much gas suddenly. This is the way the pilot had been killed the day before, I think.

I got into another one and took it up about 3,000 feet to maneuver it about. It is very quick on the ailerons; it climbs well, but it has a very slow speed, probably not over 110 to 115 miles an hour, and dives very slowly.

I think the German Fokkers are getting about 125 or 130 miles an hour and dive with great rapidity. The Sopwith Camel would be no match for them in the kind of fighting we are having at Château-Thierry, I therefore told the commanding officer of the depot that they had better send the Camels to the schools; that we would not use them on the front at that time. Dunwoody put forward his utmost efforts to get us Spads and we immediately began to obtain them from the French.

My reconnaissance across the front has convinced me that the Germans have a great supply point at Fère-en-Tardenois. Every time I have flown over it there has been a tremendous movement of German teams, temporary railroads, motor trucks, and all kinds of transport in that vicinity. The town has several large woods near it. These, I estimated, are filled with supplies and ammunition.

We are also pushing aërial night reconnaissance into that area, as are the French. Major Armengaud of the French Aviation is with General Foch at the Château Bombon, immediately behind us. He and I keep constantly in touch with each other.

Armengaud notes all the reconnaissance that we make over the front—that is, by both the French and the American Aviation—and keeps a record of it each day. In addition, he posts up a map for each day which shows where we consider the center of the German movement to be. This, Armengaud calls his cinema. It is perfectly accurate.

Armengaud estimates the Germans will attack somewhere around the middle of the month, and that when the attack comes it will be the greatest ever seen. Marshal Foch knows all about our air reconnaissance and is shown Armengaud's "cinema" every day.

As our patrols were being so badly chewed up and we were losing so many men, both in the pursuit and observation aviation, I went to Major Gérard, commanding the French Aviation, and told him that I believed our present tactics led to nothing and were destroying all our aviation, because we were spreading it out in a thin layer across the front, while the Germans acted in large groups and could puncture our thin line of patrols anywhere.

I asked him to request bombardment aviation, and proposed that with this we attack the German supply points at Fère-en-Tardenois. In this way we could mass all our bombardment and pursuit aviation together and deliver a united attack against a key point in the area which the Germans would have to defend. Otherwise their main ammunition dumps would be blown up and their supplies burned.

He agreed to this, and asked the French Army General Headquarters for bombardment aviation. They replied they had none which could be spared at that time, but forwarded the request to General Foch's headquarters.

Foch immediately asked the British if they had any bombardment aviation which they could spare. The British replied by sending a brigade of their air force to our support at once: three squadrons of bombardment airplanes and four squadrons of pursuit. It was a formidable and efficient force, and came through the air with an aviation general as commander of it.

The following day we made a combined air attack on Fère-en-Tardenois. The British bombardment attacked with tremendous valor. They came down in broad daylight to within a few hundred feet of the ground, blowing up several ammunition dumps which could be plainly seen by our ground troops.

The Germans were taken completely by surprise, and now had to stand on the defensive in the air, as this was their key point. If we blew up all their ammunition there and wrecked their supplies, their movement into the Château-Thierry area would be brought to a standstill. We had no such key point behind our front, and could therefore afford to push everything into the attack.

Unfortunately, the British lost twelve bombardment airplanes in this attack, as the Germans were concentrated over all sides. Our observation airplanes were not interfered with after this happened, as the German pursuit had to keep in the air constantly to defend the Fére-en-Tardenois area. We had found the Achilles' heel of the German position north of the Marne and had seized the initiative in the air.

One of our pilots, who had just come up, became separated from his squadron, and engaged in a free-lance patrol when he met a German directly over our infantry lines. Our man attacked with such ardor that he soon forced his opponent down, out of control. The German landed, and was seized by our infantry troops. Our pilot landed in an adjoining field.

The German saw the ship come down, and expressed a

desire to meet the American. Our pilot hurried over to get a glimpse of his prisoner, as it was his first day on the front.

When the German heard that he had been shot down by a novice, on the line for the first time, he flew into a rage. He himself had nineteen official victories to his credit.

Hardly a plane of our observation aviation has returned without having entered into combat.

July, 1918.

We are having a great deal of trouble making the ground units answer our signals from the air. They are afraid if they show any panels or smoke signals they will be seen by the enemy and result in immediate attack.

I have established my headquarters at a little place south of Coulommiers, at a country estate called Haute Feuille, owned by a family named Becker. It is a shooting box and the estate is filled with pheasants and hares. The house itself is entirely modern, very comfortably arranged and with all conveniences. I established our offices in some of the outbuildings, and it is an excellent place for us to work in.

We also have plenty of room to take care of visitors who come in either to inspect the units or on rubbernecking expeditions. The rubbernecks are a terrible nuisance and are difficult to keep off.

Our infantry troops are now having considerable influence on the combat, and some of our artillery is beginning to make itself felt. I am now getting increased cooperation from nearly everybody, and on July 5 I sent General Foulois the following letter relating to our condition at Château-Thierry:

HEADQUARTERS, AIR SERVICE,
FIRST BRIGADE

July 5, 1918.

MY DEAR FOULOIS:

I am very sorry not to be able to come in to Paris today. General Liggett has specially requested me to stay here, as we expect an attack to take place during the night. I may be able to come in tomorrow evening, but I doubt it. I am sending Lieutenant Miller with these papers, which explain themselves.

On the whole, the movement of the groups to this locality was well done, for the first time. The pursuit group was particularly well handled by its commander. I am having the airdrome shifted today so as to simplify the observation work and conform to the general scheme. I am having maps made for you of the localities. We will begin to get operations reports out tomorrow.

The supply system has functioned pretty well, but too many approvals have to be obtained for various things. For instance, to have anti-aircraft machine guns issued to a group required somebody's approval in Tours; to obtain transportation for my headquarters required somebody's approval whom I have never heard of before and who cannot be found. The result is, we have no trucks, motorcycles, or light cars. This must be simplified.

As to tactical organization, I am convinced that the brigade system is sound; that the pursuit groups should have six squadrons of twenty-four machines each; and that the combat wings should be as I outlined to you before.

Under existing conditions, the repair and supply system should be as follows:

1. Keep the machine shop trucks with the squadrons. They can be brought together by the group commanders if desired.

2. Move up your mobile parks, in accordance with the "dope" that was gotten up in Toul for pursuit and observation units, to a convenient point in their vicinity.

3. Establish an air depot behind these. Memoranda for Colonel Milling attached hereto indicate the change in tactics and instruction needed. Be careful that pilots are not sent to observation units as a punishment. We are reaping the benefits of this now in smashed Salmson airplanes.

I have sent instructions today for the Eighty-eighth Squadron to come. We need the Second Pursuit Group here very badly, and we have a place ready for it.

Several communications have come through relating

to changes of personnel, etc., in this brigade without coming through these headquarters. I think care should be taken in this respect hereafter, now that we are established.

Our losses will be quite great during the summer. They appear to be running about 80 per cent at least per month in pursuit aviation from all causes. We formerly estimated 100. The losses in airplanes will run about half as much for pursuit; for observation about one-third of this. Ample replacement should be sent to Orly, ready to come out here.

I hope you will stop by here on your way out, and let me know before you come, so that I may be here.

WILLIAM MITCHELL,
Colonel, Air Service,
Commanding First Brigade.

The same day I sent a letter to Colonel Milling, who is handling the battle training of our units in the Toul area, as to what should take place there. It is as follows:

HEADQUARTERS, AIR SERVICE
FIRST BRIGADE

July 5, 1918.

MEMORANDUM for: Colonel Milling.

1. The following measures will be taken in the battle training of units in accordance with recent developments: Ordinarily all pursuit groups will receive their information from the anti-aircraft artillery as to hostile aircraft by means of radio-telegraphy. Each group will, therefore, be equipped with radio. The information will be transmitted in cipher.

2. When we arrived here the Germans were acting in large patrols of from ten to fifteen airplanes each. We attacked them in echelons of five; *i.e.,* two patrols of five each acting together. The Germans quickly changed and adopted our methods, and as they have very fast ships and are excellently trained both as individuals and in formation, they are much more formidable than we have been used to. This, of course, was foreseen.

The proper formation for attacking their large bodies

is two squadrons acting together, each arranged in three flights of five or six airplanes in echelon. The flights in squadron to vary about 600 meters in distance and the squadrons to vary about 1,000 meters in distance. The position of the flights with respect to order in squadron may be varied from time to time; *i.e.*, either in V shape or in line. The squadron commander should fly with the center formation, whatever it may be.

The training of the individual pilots is not bad, and their ability to fight in patrols of five is fair. Whenever you have the opportunity, have the squadrons practice as indicated above. Lay special stress on prompt answers to orders for getting into the air.

3. Have them practice signals with the anti-aircraft artillery as to changing direction in accordance with the instructions already existing. Our fights have lasted from fifteen to thirty minutes within the last two days. The anti-aircraft posts can, therefore, give alerts for these fights and re-enforcements can be sent in ample time if handled promptly.

Our loss in pursuit pilots is averaging at least 80 per cent a month here. We are inflicting a little more losses on the Germans than we receive at the present. Therefore, have your squadron commanders instructed in how to make use of the replacement pilots to the best advantage. Have your squadron commanders set an example and get plenty of "pep" into their pilots, and be sure that the operations officers know the sectors well and know the Germans' tactics well and think clearly and act quickly.

4. As to observation aviation, have every measure taken with a view to a war of movement in which liaisons necessarily are of the most rudimentary character. This means the closest connections with the troops on the ground and brigade, division, and army-corps posts of command. Lay great stress on fugitive target work for the artillery and the adjustment of trench mortars.

The depth to which corps observation must operate extends to over fifteen kilometers on account of the range of the corps artillery. This requires a great deal of work at high altitude. We always find Germans here around 5,000 meters. Pick your pilots carefully for this sort of work, because many of them who are good down low are no good up there. All the ships for use at that altitude should be equipped with oxygen respirators. Observation ships should have machine guns capable of firing downward. On account of the altitude at which they have to operate, corps observation squadrons should be equipped with 120-centimeter cameras.

Night reconnaissance must be greatly developed. All routes of approach of the enemy to certain localities must be carefully studied with a view to their inspection at night. The zone of reconnaissance will cover the same areas at night as it does in the daytime; *i.e.,* the corps squadrons will cover their areas and the army squadrons their areas.

It is probable that a night squadron or a night flight, or something of that sort will have to be attached to each corps observation group, with its corresponding increment to army observation groups. Special fields will have to be reserved for this purpose, so as to prevent bombardment of the ordinary observation fields.

Train your pilots in night flying. The Sopwiths with flares under the wings are suitable for this. Balloon observers must be specialized in night observation. These are the principal points developed in the few days that we have been here.

WILLIAM MITCHELL,
Colonel, Air Service,
Commanding First Brigade.

On July 9 we had a meeting of the corps commanders of the Sixth French Army, commanded by General Degoutte, at his headquarters. The corps commanders, their chiefs of staff, Major Gérard, and I attended.

General Degoutte explained the dispositions he wished made to defend the area against the Germans in the attack which we knew was coming soon. He then asked each corps commander to explain what his dispositions were to carry out these orders.

Each one, in turn, arose and explained what he had done to meet the orders. When it came to General Liggett's turn, he arose and, in a straightforward manner, clearly and concisely stated the manner in which he had carried out his part of the program. I never felt more proud of one of our commanders, as it was the first time a great body of American troops under its own command had entered into this combat.

We are living in daily expectation of an attack, and I am doing everything in my power to get up the new airplanes with which to equip our pilots. Every day sees me more convinced that our flying men, with the excellent training they are receiving in the schools in the interior, and under the leaders that we have developed on the front, will be superior to any other airmen in the world, and it is only a question of time before we shall have the ascendancy over the Germans.

But, as things stand on this part of the front during the first half of July, I think that we are outnumbered in the air almost five to one. We have to make up this deficiency by superior strategy and tactics.

On July 14 I hurried into Paris in the afternoon to get more action about our new airplanes, as we live in hourly expectation of an attack. Masses of German troops have been moved down to their attacking positions. We do not know exactly where they will attack, but we feel sure it will be against Reims.

Next day I was getting a late dinner preparatory to starting back to my headquarters, when Donald Brown of the Red Cross came in and sat down with me. At precisely twelve-ten A.M. [July 15, 1918] we heard the reverberation of guns to the north, and, looking in that direction, we could see tremendous flashes in the sky. I was certain that the main attack of the Germans was being launched.

I told Brown if he wanted to see the greatest battle in history he could come with me. We started in my fastest automobile for my headquarters at Haute Feuille, which we reached a little before three o'clock.

The appearance of the front from this place is impossible to describe. The whole sky was lighted up by the flash of artillery on both sides. Rockets and signals were appearing everywhere; searchlight beams were sweeping the sky; the buzz of airplanes going and coming, and the noise of their bombs dropping, covered the whole of the line. We yet were uncertain where the main attack was being made.

I called up our pursuit group and observation groups on the telephone and ordered them to have everything ready to operate by daylight. Just as I finished this, Major Gérard, with Lieutenant Lafant, who had first taken me over the line in April, 1917, reached my headquarters.

Gérard was greatly perturbed. He informed me that the main German attack was on; that they were pressing the front of the Third French Army, of which we were a part; and that a great attack was being made against the Fourth French Army under General Gouraud in the Champagne. He did not know what success the Germans had had so far, but he did know that our troops were making terrific resistance at every point so as to prevent the Germans from crossing the Marne.

He told me that the orders for the aviation for the following morning had miscarried, and that the word had not reached the French Air Division in sufficient time for them to prepare for an early-morning attack. The only air troops left for this part of the front, he said, were our pursuit group, our observation squadrons, and the British brigade.

We discussed the advisability of putting up a barrage or curtain patrol along the front at daylight. This, I informed him, I would not approve of, as it would merely lead to unnecessary losses and would give us no advantage. I proposed that we hold all our air forces in readiness to act a little before daylight; that we send up our night reconnaissance at once to cover the whole front of the Army, find out what the enemy is doing, and act accordingly. This he agreed to and went back to his headquarters.

I snatched a few minutes' sleep, then went to the airdrome of the First Pursuit Group at Saintes. There I took an airplane and flew straight north until I reached La Ferté-sous-Jouarre, and then north of this to where our lines began.

The ceiling was low in places, but I saw no German airplanes whatever or any movement of troops on the ground except a general artillery fire all along the front. I turned to the right and flew up the Marne. Not a German airplane made its appearance.

As I approached Jaulgonne, I met a few Fokker airplanes,

who either did not see me or, if they did, they paid no attention to me.

Suddenly, as I rounded a turn of the river east of Dormans, I saw a great mass of artillery fire hitting the south bank of the Marne, and five bridges filled with troops marching over. I looked everywhere for German airplanes, but there were none in the sky at that time. I received no anti-aircraft fire, and apparently no attention was paid to me. I flew within 500 feet of the bridges.

I flew a little farther up the river and then turned up toward Reims. A terrific battle was going on in that vicinity and the air was full of German airplanes. I turned around and came back to the bridges. By that time a terrible combat was going on on top of the hill just south of the bridges. The opposing troops were almost together.

This is the nearest to a hand-to-hand combat of anything I have seen so far. I thought they were Americans, and later found that it was our Third Division. They are the ones that stopped the advance of the Germans at that point. I do not think they had any artillery, as I could not see any. There were now a good many German airplanes in the air and I had to be careful. I reached the airdrome of our First Pursuit Group safely, and immediately ordered the whole group to Dormans to attack the bridges, the German troops on the ground, and to clear the air over the combat between the Germans and our troops.

I then proceeded to General Liggett's headquarters at La Ferté-sous-Jouarre, and reported to him and Craig, his chief of staff, what I had seen and my estimate of the situation. I sent in a report to the headquarters of the Third French Army and Major Gérard, and communicated with Armengaud at General Foch's headquarters. This was the first definite information that was obtained that morning about the location of the bridges and the movement of the Germans.

It was now apparent in my mind that the Germans were aiming for Reims, that the movement across the Marne at Dormans was for protecting the right flank of this attack, and that their attack against the Fourth French Army in the Champagne was to protect the left flank. We heard that General Gouraud had retired from all his front lines, had allowed the Germans to occupy them without resistance, and was now counterattacking them with his whole army and making headway.

I went down to see Armengaud at General Foch's headquarters, and we went over the situation. It is quite evident that, as the Germans were attacking at the head of the salient of which the base was formed by Soissons on one side and Reims on the other, if we could get in from either side of the base we could turn the whole German position and, if successful, attack them in the rear and maybe destroy their whole army.

It was the best chance that presented itself during the war, and Marshal Foch was not slow to avail himself of it.

Obviously the place to attack was near Soissons. Our reconnaissance showed that it was not heavily held by the Germans.

The following day we were instructed to prevent German reconnaissance over our area at all costs, so we pushed our attacks again in the direction of Fère-en-Tardenois.

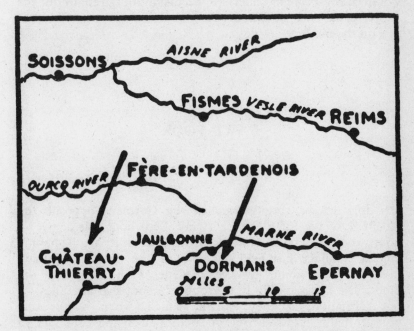

Map shows where the Third Division stopped the German advance at the bridges over the Marne near Dormans.

We were informed that our First and Second divisions, accompanied by the Moroccan Division, were to move north at night to the vicinity of Soissons and attack as soon as the movement was completed.

During the daytime, troops from various parts of the line were to move south along the roads from the vicinity of Soissons, so as to make the Germans think that re-enforcements were being sent to the right of the French Third Army and to the left of the Fourth in the vicinity of Reims.

During this same day the First and Second American divisions and the Moroccan Division were moved north at night, with no lights showing and with as great secrecy as possible, to the vicinity of Soissons.

It was an operation fraught with the greatest importance for the Allies. If it succeeded, the Germans would have to retire from the Château-Thierry salient, and before they could recover sufficiently to break through again, the American military forces, their aviation, and their ground troops would have brought such an accession of strength to the Allied cause that it would be impossible for the Germans to gain the mastery.

PART FOUR

July, 1918 (continued).

ON July 16 we counterattacked the Germans opposite the left flank of the Fifth French Army. Zero hour was at twelve noon, and our whole aviation participated in it. We had some violent combats; just held our own in fine shape. We attack in echelon by flights of five airplanes each, one after the other. The Germans fly in a group of about five airplanes—a fan formation, as they call it, which, when it hits one of our flights, spreads out on both flanks and attempts to get over, under, and on each side of it.

This seems all very well theoretically, but a spirited attack of one flight of five ships of our pursuit throws it into confusion. The succeeding flights, still holding their formation, come in one after another, and the last formed organization wins the fight. I look for the Germans to change to our tactics in a few days.

I went to sleep on the night of July 17 with great hopes for the morrow, when the attack at Soissons was to take place. German aviation, I knew, was concentrated over their main attack, centering at Reims. I had kept any great amount of aërial activity away from the vicinity of Soissons. The only fliers that had been over before were Brereton and Hazlett, who flew clear across the salient. I had preceded them the day before in a single-seater machine. Both of these trips were very hazardous and difficult to perform.

I went to bed thinking that our orders for the morrow were O. K. and that the British brigade at Ormeux and our First Pursuit Group would be available for the fight. At three-thirty in the morning I was awakened by Major Gérard, who was again in great perturbation. The orders had been all mixed up and the British air brigade had been directed to attack in the Reims area, which could not be changed at that time.

This left our First Pursuit Group as the only air organization to cover the front on the day of our most important attack. I told Major Gérard that we could handle the matter, but that the whole group would have to act together, and, in addition, we would put in all our observation aviation, to lend what assistance they could.

He agreed to this entirely, and when dawn broke, off went every airplane that we had to clear the air over our comrades on the ground in the most important operation during our participation in the European War, if not in the whole war since the beginning.

Fortunately, the Germans were taken by surprise, and we kept the sky clear while our splendid divisions, the First and Second, with the Moroccan Division between them, broke the German line west of Soissons.

It may seem strange to some that a great soldier like General Ludendorff had denuded that most important part of his line. It is one of the rudiments of military strategy, when one is acting out from the point of a salient, to hold the base of the salient strongly, because if that is broken the enemy gets behind you, which is fatal.

I have been told that General Ludendorff, the German Chief of Staff, counted his troops that were in certain areas according to the number of battalions. A battalion normally has about 1,000 men, of which about 500 or 600 can be depended on to fight on the line. The German battalions, however, were reduced to a strength of from 100 to 200 men in many cases, so that no more than 50 or 100 men were available for duty.

Our splendid troops have broken the line. Our First and Second divisions are now first-class fighting troops. They have had a great deal of experience and a tremendous amount of training. They can stand the losses and, with adequate leaders, will not fail us. The Forty-second Division is close behind them, and soon there will be others.

I flew over the area during the attack in the afternoon. The Germans began to get a few airplanes over, but it was too late. The next day I noticed a great deal of German movement throughout the salient, and I was sure that a German retreat was to be made.

The attacks kept up at Soissons. I went up to see the condition of the First and Second divisions as they came out of the line. Although very tired, they showed all the characteristics of good troops. They held their formations; there was little straggling. Their equipment was in fair condition; their officers carried themselves in splendid manner.

There was no doubt in my mind now that the Germans were retreating as rapidly as possible, and marching mostly at night so as to get away from our air reconnaissance and attacks.

Our balloons under Major Paegelow were doing especially good work. While the troops on the ground did not know much about using them, Paegelow always had them ready and always up with the troops, and we got a great deal of information from them. As our aviation was so far outnumbered by the Germans, I knew that we would have lots of balloons shot down, and made Paegelow provide two spare balloons immediately behind each one that was on the line.

One of our balloon companies had an observer jump five

times in a parachute in one day—three times out of his burning balloon and twice when it looked as if his balloon would surely be burned. I shall recommend him for the D.S.C.

We had been issued only two anti-aircraft machine guns for the balloon companies. Later I obtained four, but now I wanted to get as many as I could. I told Paegelow that he did not have enough machine guns with his balloon companies. He asked me where he should get them, and I told him I did not care where he got them—that I wanted them there by the next day.

Imagine my surprise when I visited one of the balloon companies the next day and counted thirty-two machine guns around the balloon which could put up a terrific barrage. Upon looking at them I saw that they were German Maxims, really better guns than we have, with corrector sights for anti-aircraft fire. Old Paegelow had found and captured a machine-gun depot, and had immediately appropriated all that he could possibly carry away in every kind of vehicle obtainable. These are the kind of men to have on the front.

I went down to Bombon, General Foch's headquarters. Armengaud was elated. All of the data that we had gathered from the air had proved to be correct. The point of attack as shown by our aërial reconnaissance was exact and we had been able to tell within a few hours when the attack would come.

Now General Foch is going to keep hitting at different points all along the line, so as to keep the Germans occupied at the same time, and, in addition, get together a mass of maneuver which he can hurl at any place required.

We now are sure that the Germans are on the run. They escaped our trap at Soissons because we could not get into the salient quite fast enough. I consider the Battle of Soissons one of the decisive battles of the war. The first was the Battle of the Marne, in which it was determined that the French Republic could not be conquered during the first onslaught; second was the Battle of Tannenberg, in which the Germans destroyed the Russian military power. And now the Battle of Soissons, which has thrown back the German advance at the most critical time in the whole war. From now on there is no question that we can build up sufficient military strength to crush the central empires, unless peace intervenes before.

Foulois recently has been coming up frequently and giving all the assistance possible. Patrick is having round-table conferences in Paris. I attended one, and was favorably impressed with what was done. There were some really practical men sitting there.

Dunwoody and Major Satterfield from Buffalo, New York, are doing wonderfully. Satterfield never misses a trick. Their whole principle is to get the stuff that we need to us. When we tell them we want something, they do not say there is something else just as good—they get it. General Pershing is giving us more and more support.

I have just heard of poor Bolling's death and how it occurred. When he had been stripped of all his authority in Paris, he applied for service on the front. We had determined that as soon as he became familiar enough with the work he would be made Chief of Air Service of the Second Army Corps. To perfect himself in the work, Bolling kept up his flying eagerly and obtained permission to go to the British front.

He proceeded there with a small automobile and a chauffeur. During the March offensive, when the Fifth British Army was destroyed by the Germans, Bolling hurried out to the front to see what was going on. The British air force alone was holding up the German advance along the sector of the front by attacking the German troops on the ground as they came forward and stopping them, which was giving a respite to the fugitives of the British Fifth Army in their retreat.

Hurrying toward what he supposed to be the line still held by the British troops, he ran squarely into an outpost of Germans. They called on him to surrender, but rather than do this he jumped in a shell hole beside the road and defended himself with his pistol. The chauffeur was overpowered and captured. Bolling refused to give himself up, and after shooting several Germans was himself killed.

On July 25 General Foulois sent me the following letter, which rather surprised me. Foulois certainly was trying hard at this time to do everything that he could, and we were supporting him from our end.

          France, July 25, 1918.

From: Chief of Air Service, First Army.
To: Commander-in-Chief, American E. F.
Subject: Assignment of Colonel William Mitchell as Chief of Air Service, First Army.

1. I recommend that Colonel William Mitchell, Air Service, be assigned to duty as Chief of Air Service, First Army.

2. In connection with this recommendation, I wish to bring to your attention the most efficient service of Colonel Mitchell during the past month in the organization, battle training, general supervision, and guidance of the Air Service units which have been operating with the Franco-American troops in the Château-Thierry area.

These units had had but a limited amount of tactical training in the quiet sector of the Toul area, when they were ordered to the Château-Thierry area. The unit commanders, although excellent officers, and eager and willing to learn, had had no experience in major tactical offensive operations, such as were encountered immediately upon their arrival in the Château-Thierry area.

Colonel Mitchell, as Commanding Officer of the First Air Brigade, and as the representative of the Chief of Air Service, First Army, was directed to exercise technical supervision over these units, and, if necessary, in emergencies to exercise tactical supervision in order to absolutely insure efficient results. I am glad to say that the technical and tactical supervision exercised over these units by Colonel Mitchell has resulted in a minimum loss of life, a maximum effective use of material available, and a high fighting spirit of morale which will be most beneficial in establishing the standard of efficiency for all new Air Service units now organizing and to be organized in the future.

          B. D. FOULOIS
          Brigadier General, S. C.

On July 27 I was formally notified of my appointment as

Chief of Air Service of the First Army, to take command of the air troops. I was ready for this, because for over a year I had been working on just what we would do in that eventuality. I moved my headquarters up to La Ferté-sous-Jouarre. The last days of July were spent in making arrangements for organizing the Air Service of the First Army.

Although there were many things left to be desired, I felt that our work at Château-Thierry had been remarkable; I mean that of the ground troops as well as the air troops. The Germans are now thrown back, and will have to remain on the defensive because their available reserves for attacking are used up. They still could retire, greatly shorten their front, and again get together a mass of maneuver for striking; but I believe that they will allow us to attack and use ourselves up, if such a thing is possible, before moving to the rear.

This war on the ground—that is, with the armies—is an endless performance. The armies will fight for months, lose hundreds of thousands of men, billions of dollars' worth of equipment, and one or the other will have advanced a mile or two. This isn't war—it is a slaughterhouse!

The Germans have been getting very active in the Toul sector. They must have strong suspicions that our American Army will begin to operate in that area. The other night they destroyed or damaged twenty-four British airplanes in the airdrome at Ochey.

This place has the usual peacetime arrangement of airplane hangars, set all in a line. Each of them has five or six bombardment airplanes inside of them. The hangars are made of galvanized iron. The sides are heaped up with sandbags to a height of about six or seven feet, to prevent the splinters of bombs getting into them. What happened was as follows:

Each night the British airplanes went over the front on a raid. When they came back they would give a signal with a certain kind of rocket to identify themselves. Then the airdrome would be lighted up and the airplane would land. The British did not change the signal for three nights. The Germans, of course, were watching it all the time.

On the third night a German airplane came over, gave the

British signal for landing, the airdrome was lighted up, and the German came right down over the hangars, dropping bombs all along the line.

In some cases the hangars were blown down and the machines entirely destroyed inside of them. In other cases a bomb punctured a small hole through the roof of the hangar, exploded on the ground inside, blew all the linen covering of the wings off of the airplanes, and filled the whole hangar full of holes.

Colonel Milling and Major Hall had a narrow escape the other evening not far from Toul. They were going along the road in their automobile, with a chauffeur and a couple of British officers, when a German airplane espied them and fired a few machine-gun bullets at them. They could be very plainly seen at night, as the road is so white.

As they descended a hill the right hind wheel had a puncture, and they stopped beside the road. They lighted a light for just an instant to see how to get the wheel off. But in that instant the German airplane saw them and dropped two small bombs. One exploded in a ditch about ten feet off and did no damage; the other exploded a little closer, and hit virtually every member of the party, mortally wounding the chauffeur, who died the next day.

I have just heard that Allan Winslow is reported missing. We have sent Wentworth, a cousin of his, up to see what he can find, because we think he was shot down somewhere near our front line. I am very sorry to lose Winslow. He was the first American to shoot down a German airplane, and has done well with us ever since.

August, 1918.

Beginning with the first of August, we rapidly pushed forward our preparations for assembling the greatest air force that the world has ever seen. It was evident that, as soon as we Americans began to act as an independent army, the Germans would concentrate their whole air force on us for the purpose of demoralizing all our ground troops by seizing and holding dominion of the air over us.

I estimated that, within three days after we attacked, the Germans could concentrate very nearly 2,000 airplanes against us. I therefore decided to assemble a force of 2,000 to cover our initial attack, no matter where it might be. I immediately took up the matter, through Armengaud, with

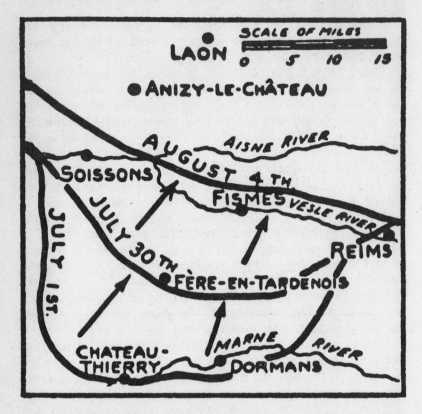

Map showing the territory around Soissons where the First and Second divisions went over in 1918.

the French, to find out what they could spare. General Foch approved everything that we put forward, in principle, and our work went rapidly on.

I now began to get the old staff officers that I had trained together, particularly Colonel T. D. Milling. He is the best Chief of Staff that I have ever seen in any service.

Different commanding officers use their chiefs of staff in different ways. I always have my Chief of Staff coordinate the various staff sections and see that the machine functions properly. When I am commanding, I always draw up my own orders for the military operations of the fighting units, and personally check the sending and receipt by the unit commander of their special orders.

When orders are not obeyed, it is usually the commanding officer that is at fault. Either the orders have not been delivered or they are so written that nobody can understand them. I always kept an officer at my headquarters, whose name I will not mention, to whom I had read all the orders. If he could understand them, anybody could. He was not particularly bright, but he was one of the most valuable officers I had for that reason.

On August 4 I drove up to Château-Thierry, along the road on the north side of the Marne. I was tremendously impressed by the looks of Vaux on the ground. Brereton's observation aviation had conducted the artillery shoot against this town. I have never seen greater destruction anywhere. Every house was down; the débris had to be blasted with dynamite out of the road to open it.

As I approached Château-Thierry, I saw some fine infantry coming up the road. Soon I met my old friend McCoy. We stopped to have a few words, and I asked him what organization these fine troops that were passing belonged to and where they had come from. He said they had just come out of the line on the Vesle, and that it was the Sixty-ninth New York, which he had the honor of commanding.

I had some work to do in Château-Thierry. As I came out of a building I heard some trumpets blowing for a march past. I looked across the square, and there was General Degoutte reviewing the Sixty-ninth New York, with McCoy beside him.

This gallant regiment has had a fine history in our great battles, both in the Civil War and this one. They can have no better commanding officer than McCoy. He should have been made a general long ago.

This regiment is composed entirely of Irishmen from the East Side of New York, and always has been.

In our former wars the replacements for it have come from their own section of the city and have also been Irish; but I am told that in this war, replacements come from anywhere they can get them, and that most of the recruits sent up are Jews.

The combination of Irish and Jews seems to be doing pretty well.

Our officers and men are beginning to get that warrior look which comes only from contact with a strong enemy. It is quickly lost when troops are withdrawn from the front for a considerable period, and comes back again only after hard fighting.

On August 13 I flew my Spad from the Château-Thierry area to Neufchâteau, where I established my headquarters and staff. On the night of my departure the Germans unmercifully bombed the railroad station which was just across from my headquarters at La Ferté-sous-Jouarre, practically blew it up, and smashed my fine old house all to pieces. Our staff now began to prepare for the coming of our great air host.

This work fell primarily on Captain Joralemon, my equipment officer. Joralemon is a mining engineer and had one of the high positions in the great copper mines in Sonora in Mexico. He has the greatest job that any air supply officer has ever had, because he has to prepare for the coming of a maximum of 2,000 airplanes of fourteen or fifteen kinds, requiring spare parts for each, supplying them with gasoline and oil, guns and ammunition of all sorts, bombs of eight or ten sizes and kinds.

Each airdrome has to be thoroughly renovated and repaired, housing provided for all the men and pilots, and Captain Marvel, our signal officer, has to install an entirely independent telephone system and radiotelegraph net to handle our communications.

Armengaud of the French service is a tower of strength to us, and I shall make him my Assistant Chief of Staff for Operations. He smooths everything out between us and the French service. We have two Italian squadrons also. We have arranged with my old friend General Trenchard, the splendid commander of the British Independent Air Force, to cooperate with us with his bombardment force of about 100 ships.

On August 28 I formally assumed command of the Air Service of the First Army. This was the first definite American command which was organized for grand operations in our history. I moved my headquarters up to Ligny-en-Barrois on August 27. Lieutenant Miller had prepared for the movement. We had taken over a public-school building as our headquarters.

I had procured a wonderful relief map of the whole St. Mihiel salient that we were about to attack. It had been made up by the French balloon companies operating in this area, and had been the work of several years. I had gotten the various pieces and put them together.

It occupied a floor space of about twelve by twelve feet. Each hill, wood, road, detached house, large building, railroad, railroad yard, ravine—and in fact every incident of the terrain—was remarkably depicted.

This, combined with my intimate knowledge of the country, derived in the first place from studying it for many years, and now from flying over it with both French and American observers with me, made me feel that I knew this part of the world as well as any man living, and better probably than any Frenchman himself.

We were still having a terrible time getting suitable airplanes. Colonel Hall, a motor manufacturer from California, and one of the designers of the Liberty motor, has been given the job of technical development in our supply service.

I had met Colonel Hall several months before, when he had been a member of a party of joy riders, but paid little attention to him at that time, as I thought that as soon as he got through with seeing what he wanted, he would go back to the United States and tell about it, the way all the rest of them did. But it was different with Hall. He came here to work, and work he did, with tremendous intelligence and energy.

My staff is working well. Colonel De Witt, of G-4 of the Army, is handling the question of the shipment of our supplies in a masterly manner. I think De Witt is probably the ablest officer on the army staff. Nothing ever seems to go wrong with him. That means a lot in this kind of war, where nearly the whole game is a question of the number of pounds of supplies that can be sent up. De Witt's routing along the roads and railroads seems never to miscarry.

General Pershing now is in high spirits. We are getting our American Army together; and our air people—who for a long time have felt that Pershing did not know, or care to know, very much about aviation—are beginning to change their minds, as he is helping us in every way possible.

I guess he could not swallow the whole hog to begin with— had to take it easy; but it put us back a good many months. One has to expect that in the organization of a new outfit, and from now on I hope he will do better, and I am sure he will if we deliver the goods.

The closing days of August saw us assembling the greatest army the United States has ever seen, to do battle on European soil. Thousands upon thousands of men fill every road, while all means of transport are bringing the tremendous amount of supplies they require.

September, 1918.

The 1st of September saw my headquarters permanently organized, and a force of 1,476 airplanes and twenty balloons, under my command, concentrating to join battle with the Germans. Thirty thousand officers and men handle the airplanes. They are disposed on fourteen main flying fields and a great many substations, while three large supply points handle the material for the Americans, the French, the British, and the Italians.

It is the greatest concentration of air power that has ever taken place. It is the first time in history in which an air force, cooperating with an army, is to act according to a broad strategical plan, which contemplates not only facilitating the advance of the ground troops, but spreading fear and consternation into the enemy's line of communications, his replacement system, and the cities and towns behind them which supply our foe with the sinews of war.

General Trenchard of the British Air Force, my old friend of the early days of the war, and one of the greatest figures in the whole European contest, whether on the ground or in the air, has been relieved of command of the air forces acting with the British Army, because of his pronounced views on the subject of how air power should be organized.

He stanchly held that it should be separate from the army and navy and be used as an independent force—which is absolutely right—and accordingly he has been assigned to head the Independent Air Force, an organization designed to bomb the interior cities of Germany, where lie their manufacturing and supply resources.

In addition to the American, French, and British units, I have some squadrons of Italian bombardment aviation who do all they can in their sphere. Here we are, a force of four nations, acting together with no discord, misunderstanding, jealousy, or attempt to shirk or escape the maximum duty or losses which may be required. Such a thing could not have occurred with ground troops. I say this because the game on the ground is such an old one. The element of novelty and development has ceased to exist in it.

Another thing that lends strength to our association and understanding of each other is the fact that I have had our officers study the methods, ways of doing things, and even personality of the officers composing the air forces that are acting with us. When foreign officers join us I put them right in our organization, give them responsibilities and duties to perform.

Armengaud is one of them. Most of the time when I reconnoiter in my two-seater airplane I put Armengaud in the back seat. He is one of the best observers that I have ever seen—cool, observing, brave, and resourceful. The other French officers that I have at my headquarters have been carefully selected also, and not taken by me on the recommendation of someone else. They were taken only on my approval after I had seen them work.

Most of the officers on our General Staff have no appreciation of what this great air force means. There are some marked exceptions to this. Not one, however, except Major Bowditch, has shown any inclination to go up in the air and see what is going on.

PART FIVE

September, 1918.

WE are now able to bomb the communications of the enemy, so that we hope to hold up their movement to such an extent as to allow our ground troops to capture great numbers of them, which we can do by attacking and bombing their wagon trains, motor trucks, and railroads, piling them up so that the roads cannot be cleared away, and destroying road centers where the roads go through towns so that quick marching cannot be accomplished.

We have three conditions to face: one, to provide accurate information for the infantry and adjustment of fire for the artillery of the ground troops; second, to hold off the enemy air forces from interfering with either our air or ground troops; and, third, to bomb the back areas so as to stop the supplies for the enemy and hold up any movement along his roads.

The shape of the front—that is, the St. Mihiel salient—furnishes an interesting situation. It projects into our line in the shape of a horseshoe, rather a sharp one at the toe, to be sure. This point of the toe is located at the city of St. Mihiel. The Germans pushed in here in 1915 and occupied it in an attempt to isolate Verdun and surround it so as to cause its surrender.

It must be remembered that the most direct line of advance from Germany into France is through Coblenz, Treves, Verdun, Nancy, and then straight toward Lyons, where the centers of population and factories of France are located.

Conversely, if we can advance into Germany by way of Treves and Coblenz, we also shall have the shortest line through this great gateway into the country of the Teutons. Now our American Army, acting under its own chiefs and holding its own sector of the line, is charged with the duty of advancing into the Treves gap and, by pushing on, to threaten this great open portal into Germany.

No better mission could be given us. It is a difficult one on account of the ground lying to the north of us, particularly in the Argonne Forest; but with our fresh troops, not yet war tired, and with the great force which we are capable of assembling before many months go by, we have the post of honor of the whole campaign.

Certainly the Europeans would not have liked to give us a place of such importance in this contest; but, reduced to the last extremity of their defense by the onslaught of the Germans, they have had to gracefully acknowledge that we now hold the whip hand, and if the war is to be won by the Allies, it is the Americans who are going to win it.

At most places the line is more or less straight, and the Air Service acts out from it more or less homogeneously all along the front. Now we are attacking a "salient," so I intend to change the ordinary procedure and employ massed air attacks against the vital points in the enemy's rear. In this case we can hit first from one side of the salient and then from the other.

In the present case I shall have a preponderance in the air for at least two days before the Germans can concentrate. I have, therefore, issued orders to the French Air Division that they will attack entirely by brigades, nothing smaller. There are two brigades of about 400 airplanes each in the division. One brigade will habitually attack twice a day on the right of the salient, entering it from west of Pont-à-Mousson. The bombardment will attack Vigneulles, Conflans, and Briey.

At the time their gas is beginning to run out, the Second Brigade of the Air Division will attack the same places from the left of the salient, crossing the lines in the vicinity of Génicourt and Fort Haudainville. In this way, while the Germans are resisting one of our brigades and fighting it, I shall catch them in the rear with the other brigade.

Our bombardment wing, consisting of the Second and Third Pursuit Groups, with the bombardment group, will act out from the head of the salient and will attack Vigneulles. We have done everything we can with this new bombardment organization, but they have not yet had the experience required to make them proficient.

Our bombardment group is not in good condition. It is poorly commanded, the morale is weak, and it will take some time to get it on its feet. This is largely due to the fact that when I was away in Château-Thierry the Ninety-sixty Squadron was left behind in the Toul area.

A certain major, who was then in command of one of the air squadrons, flew over into Germany with what ships he had available for duty.

He lost his way in the fog and landed in Germany with every ship intact. Not one ship was burned or destroyed, and the Germans captured the whole outfit.

This is the most glaring exhibition of worthlessness that we have had on the front.

The Germans sent back a humorous message which was dropped on one of our airdromes. It said:

> We thank you for the fine airplanes and equipment which you have sent us, but what shall we do with the Major?

I know of no other performance in any air force that was as reprehensible as this.

Needless to say, we did not reply about the Major, as he was better off in Germany at that time than he would have been with us.

The day for the attack drew near. Joralemon had done wonderful work in locating our great air host, preparing its airdromes, and getting its supplies. Colonel De Witt, G-4, of the General Staff, had helped us to the limit. On September 7 the French Air Division reported and took its place.

We moved the air forces in to their airdromes with the greatest secrecy possible so as not to let the Germans know how many airplanes we were assembling. We were careful not to make too great a display over the front; but, on the other hand, we kept our pursuit patrols working up as high as they could go, about 20,00 feet, so as to prevent German reconnaissance.

In our advance airdromes, such for instance as at Souilly, I had camouflage or fake hangars constructed with fake airplanes in front, so that if the Germans took pictures of them it would look as if a certain number of aircraft were there. Each day I had the position of these camouflage airplanes changed.

I issued orders, among others, to the Eighty-eighth Squadron, commanded by Major Christy, to occupy the airdrome at Souilly. They were to come up from Luxeuil near Belfort, and arrive at Souilly just before dark, so as to put their airplanes into the hangars immediately and in this way escape observation from the enemy. During the night of September 9 I had real hangars put up exactly where the camouflage hangars had been.

In every other case the organizations, flying low, arrived just before dark and immediately hid themselves. Christy, however, apparently did not get the spirit of the order. He arrived with his squadron in broad daylight, leading it himself, lined it up on the field, then took his own ship with the best observer and actually made a reconnaissance away over Metz, and got away with it.

He was lucky not to have been killed, but it disclosed our whole position at Souilly. The enemy then knew exactly what was there. It was a very brave act, but absolutely the wrong thing to do. I told Christy what I thought of it. (Christy never did anything like that again; in fact, he developed into one of the best commanders that we had on the front.)

September 12 had been decided upon as the day of our grand attack. It was the greatest army ever assembled under the American flag—400,000 men with about 3,000 cannon facing the enemy. Our air force consisted of nearly, 1,500 airplanes.

Of course, the Germans knew that we were going to attack them in the St. Mihiel salient. Their power of offensive and initiative passed after the battle at Soissons. St. Mihiel was a dangerous place for them to hold; in fact, they could not; all they could do was to delay our operations.

They, therefore, had no intention of holding it, and had put in, in addition to a few of their first-line organizations, a lot of second-line troops and Austrians, in which were included many Honvéd (Hungarian) regiments.

In my personal reconnaissance with Major Armengaud over the lines on September 10, I noticed considerable movement

to the rear, which indicated that the Germans were withdrawing from the St. Mihiel salient. What was my surprise and
consternation to find at the meeting of General Pershing's
staff, on the evening before the attack, that our chief engineer recommended that we delay the attack because there
had been considerable rain.

This, he said, held up our light railways used for getting
up artillery ammunition. The question of adequate water for
some of the troops would be difficult, and a thousand and
one things which could not be done were mentioned.

I was surprised to see that several officers present agreed.
I was the junior member of the staff, and when it got to me
for my opinion, I told them very plainly that I knew the

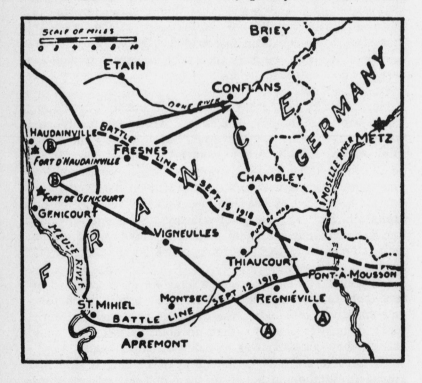

*Map shows how the Allied fliers caught the Germans first
from one side, then the other. (A) The planes attacking from
the southeast. (B) Those attacking from around Génicourt.
The dotted line shows the ground taken by the doughboys.*

Germans were withdrawing from the St. Mihiel salient, as I had seen them personally; that our troops were now in position for the attack and were keyed up to it. Furthermore, I said, there was not going to be much of a battle at St. Mihiel; our troops might be better off without artillery, as they would probably shoot a good many of our own men anyway; and all we had to do was to jump on the Germans, and the quicker we did it, the better.

General Pershing smiled and ordered that we attack.

On September 11 I assembled the officers from every major organization of the Air Service within our great force—British, French, Italians, and Americans. I read them their orders.

The morning of September 12 dawned dark and cloudy, with intermittent rain. Clouds hung low and the visibility was very poor. Nevertheless, our Air Service, with that of our Allies, went over the lines, and I was much pleased with the fact that virtually no German airplanes got over our ground troops.

We forced the German airmen to fight away back of Vigneulles and Conflans, thirty miles away from our ground troops. We had many combats at these places during the day. On September 13 we could see that the enemy was concentrating all his available air power against us because he was losing too many prisoners. The Germans did not care whether we took the St. Mihiel salient or not, but they did not want to lose a lot of prisoners and equipment.

Our air force, however, by attacking their transportation trains, railroads, and columns on the roads, piled them up with débris so that it was impossible for many of their troops to get away quickly, resulting in their capture by our infantry.

The British, under General Trenchard, tore into their airdromes, smashed up their hangars, and forced them to fight at all points.

By September 14 the German Air Service began to appear in great force and we had a tremendous number of combats. There was one fight which I wish to mention particularly, because it illustrates the terrific destructive power of pursuit aviation when acting against bombardment aviation.

On September 14 one of our bombardment squadrons belonging to a French group failed, on account of poor visibility in cloudy weather, to meet the pursuit aviation that was detailed to protect it. Nevertheless it proceeded to bombard the objective.

There were eighteen airplanes in the squadron, fifteen being two-seaters and three of them being three-seaters. The three-seaters were equipped with six guns each, and, as far as volume of gunfire was concerned, were the most powerful airplanes on the Western Front. They were unable to maneuver as rapidly as the single-seaters, however.

The three-seaters were supposed to be for the protection of the two-seaters; that is, these powerfully gunned airplanes were expected to fight off the enemy pursuit while the bombers concentrated their whole attention on dropping bombs on the targets.

The squadron flew in a V formation. One of the great three-seaters was on each flank and one in the opening behind. When this squadron crossed the line on the way to its objective, it was passed by a patrol of twelve German pursuit airplanes, flying one behind the other, about 500 meters above it.

The German patrol deployed in line formation behind the bombardment squadron. Four of the enemy airplanes attacked the three-seater which was behind, and sent it down in flames. The other eight kept up a long-range fire at the squadron so as to derange its aim while dropping its bombs on the city of Conflans. At the same time, anti-aircraft artillery opened fire at the vanguard of the squadron, while the German pursuit ships attacked the rear.

While anti-aircraft guns failed to hit any of the airplanes, their bursting shells allowed the German pursuit organizations, which were now concentrating for an attack on the squadron, to see where they were.

All the bombs were dropped on the objective and the return flight was started to our lines. Just as the turn was made, a fresh enemy pursuit squadron came up, immediately deployed, and attacked the rearmost plane and shot the observer through the leg. He continued the battle, however, and hit one enemy plane, which fell in flames.

The formation was now well on its way back, when a third enemy squadron attacked from in front and to the left. The bombing squadron was now being attacked from underneath, above, and on the same level.

The great, lumbering bombing machines huddled together as a flight of geese might when attacked by falcons, the pursuit airplanes diving at them from all directions, firing their machine guns, then zooming up in the air or turning over on their backs at a speed of about 200 miles an hour, taking an erratic course to avoid the fire of the big ships, and then resuming their position for attack again.

By this time the big three-seater protection plane on the left had been shot in one of its engines and started slipping down. Immediately when it left the formation it was jumped on by three German machines. In a moment it was shot to pieces and disappeared in flames.

Fighting now had become terrific. More German machines were constantly joining their comrades. the signals made by the artillery projectiles bursting in the air, and the radio on the ground, told the German aviators that our bombardment squadron had no pursuit protection and was an easy victim.

The attacks of the German pursuit ships were carried on up to within fifty feet of the bombardment planes.

The next airplane to be hit was No. 13, a two-seater, which caught fire and dropped its movable gasoline tank. It dived at a sharp angle, turned over on its back about 200 meters below the squadron, lost its left wing, and then crashed to the ground.

At this same moment a German pursuit ship was shot down, on fire. No. 2 bombardment airplane was hit in the gasoline tank in the upper wing, and caught fire; but the machine, flaming like a torch, kept its position in the formation. The machine gunner was magnificent in his courage, fighting the hostile airplanes while the flames slowly crept up around him. The plane continued to fly for about 200 meters, leaving behind it a trail of fire about twice as long as the ship itself.

Pilot and observer by this time were consumed, and the airplane dived to its doom. At about that time a German Fokker plane, diving vertically with its engine full on, lost both its wings. Now the whole right wing of the squadron had been shot down and a rearrangement of formation was made so as to get the remaining machines into V formation again.

Machines Nos. 9 and 14 were then both hit at the same time, No. 14 catching fire. The pilot of No. 14 stretched out his arms toward the sky, and, waving his hand and saying farewell to the remainder of the squadron, went to eternity. No. 9 machine disappeared, and as it did so an additional German pursuit machine retired from the combat, crippled.

No. 15 machine was now having a hard time keeping up with the formation. Its gasoline tank had been perforated by bullets, its aileron control cut, and its rudder hit. However, it kept up.

By this time the squadron had come back to our lines, and was joined and protected by our pursuit aviation. The combat in its intensity lasted for forty minutes, and of eighteen airplanes which had constituted the squadron only five remained.

Most of the crews were wounded and their planes perforated in all parts by bullets. They had never once broken their formation or failed to obey the orders of their leader. They furnished an example of military precision and bravery which is required of all airmen.

(These pilots were not equipped with parachutes, which might have saved many a good man, nor did they have radios with which to call for assistance to their comrades not far off. In those days we did not have such things. Today it is inexcusable to send men into combat without these two great protective measures.)

I mention this battle to show the character of training that is necessary for our people in the air. Combats of this kind during intense operations are a daily occurrence.

The Battle of St. Mihiel was really over on the first day, and every objective had been accomplished. I was glad to see that our tanks did so well, because I am convinced that in the future the tank will be the only means of advancing on the ground against a well intrenched and determined enemy. George Patton rode into St. Mihiel on the back of one of his tanks away ahead of any other ground troops in the vicinity. This is the kind of stuff that we need.

We have won a great victory at St. Mihiel. We have actually advanced about two or three miles on the ground. We have not had to move any of our airdromes or to change any of our air arrangements. The Army might fight for a month and not get too far away from the support of our present air-craft locations. This is not getting to the interior of Germany. What does it amount to, except killing thousands of our men and the enemy's?

The tanks are growing in importance every day. The British obtained a great victory on August 8 by a tank attack. The headquarters of German divisions were captured even before the alarm reached them.

Never has a ground attack succeeded so well as did this one, and I hope that our Staff will not prevent an ade-quate development of our tank service, just because it is something new.

As soon as our battle was over we began preparations for moving into the Argonne. Our green troops did all sorts of things that they shouldn't, some of which required de-cisive action.

The following order of September 16 is amusing, as it shows how easily the Germans obtained information about our troops:

HEADQUARTERS FIRST ARMY
AMERICAN EXPEDITIONARY FORCES,
FRANCE

16 September, 1918.

FROM: Chief of Staff, First Army, A.E.F.
TO: Corps Commanders, First Army, and Commanders Army Units, First Army, A.E.F.
SUBJECT: Violations of Orders.

1. Certain uncoded messages sent in violation of G.O. No. 103, c. s., G.H.Q., A.E.F., by a unit of this Com-mand during exercises in a back area, and intercepted by a control station of the First Army, could have been, and probably were, intercepted by the enemy, furnishing him with the identification of the unit and its location. Corps and Division Commanders are cautioned to make full use of their listening-in sets and control stations to detect violations of the General Order mentioned, with the view of preventing valuable information being given to the enemy, as well as with the view of taking disci-plinary action against the offenders.

2. It has been reported that during the recent offensive by the First Army certain prisoners were robbed of jewelry, money, and other personal belongings. Stringent measures will be taken by all concerned to prevent any further recurrence of such disgraceful conduct, and commanding officers will be held strictly responsible for the discipline of their units in this connection.

By command of
GENERAL PERSHING.

Our balloons did very well in the St. Mihiel battle. Although not used to the extent that they should have been by the ground troops, they rendered splendid service under Paegelow.

The observers in the baskets showed great bravery in remaining aloft under all conditions, night and day, and in some cases, where their balloons were burned by hostile attacks, jumped from their baskets in parachutes.

The enemy balloons, however, although they did little actual good to their troops, were a source of constant irritation to our ground troops. If a soldier on the ground sees any hostile aircraft in the air, no matter how impotent they may be, he at once conceives the idea that everything he does is seen and immediately reported, and, as a result, the enemy can direct his artillery fire against the reserves that are coming up from behind to help him.

Aircraft really exert an uncanny influence—on new troops particularly, and even on old ones—and quite rightly, because many of these things are so. The balloons, however, can see much less than airplanes.

In view of this comment about the German balloons bothering our ground troops so much, I called up Major Hartney, Commander of our First Pursuit Group, and had him come to my headquarters.

I told him that the orthodox way of attacking balloons by approaching them in various directions, and then pushing the attack under cover of the sun or of the forest, or some other method of obscuring the approach of the actual attacking airplanes, was pretty well understood by the Germans.

I mentioned to him that at night the balloons were pulled down to the ground and remained in their nests, and that they arose early in the morning with their envelopes damp and, therefore, would not burn readily when hit by our small .30-caliber flaming bullets. In the afternoon, as the sun is in the west, we have to go pretty far into the enemy's country to approach the balloons under its protection.

I told Hartney to go back and figure out a new way of destroying the balloons and that I did not care how he did it.

Hartney, who is an enthusiastic and able man, kept cocking his head from one side to the other, saying, "Precisely, precisely," as I gave him the instructions; but all of the time he was thinking how it would be possible to devise methods which had not been tried in the last three years.

The next morning, September 18, Hartney told me that he had a solution. Upon returning to his group, he had gone and looked at the position of various balloons, and had also sent some selected pilots to do the same thing. They also had discovered the ground nests of several German balloons.

Hartney's solution of the problem was to go out with only two pilots, one to stay above to protect the lower one. The lower one was to fly along close to the ground and shoot the balloon in its nest, just at dusk or even after dark.

Accordingly, Hartney equipped the airplanes of Lieutenants Wehner and Luke with eleven-mm. or .45-caliber machine guns, which fire a large flaming bullet. He told me that he would attack that evening at dusk, and for me to look over toward the place where the German balloon was. If I saw a large fire, it would indicate that the balloon had been successfully attacked and was burning.

I did so, and exactly at the time appointed the fire occurred. Later another one occurred.

That evening Hartney called me up and said that Luke and Wehner had destroyed two balloons, and in addition Luke had shot down an enemy airplane just south of Verdun. He had come down close to the ground, where the airplane fell, so as to make sure of the capture of the pilot. This was indeed wonderful work.

I told Hartney to continue to destroy all the German balloons, and he responded: "Yes, sir; there won't be one left on the front in a few days."

This proved to be almost correct. The Germans moved all their balloons back and put dummy balloons up, with nobody in them except a straw figure, to try and divert our attention. These they surrounded with great numbers of machine guns on the ground, which they hoped would shoot down our planes, lured to the dummy balloons.

The Germans did not pull the dummies down to earth when we came near them, but left them in the air, hoping in this way to fool our people.

Unfortunately, Wehner was killed almost immediately.

Luke, acting alone without Wehner, was shot down in enemy territory, and unfortunately was killed while defending himself with his pistol. He had obtained more victories than any other pilot during the time he was on the front.

Our problem in the Argonne is quite different from what it was at St. Mihiel. There we had a salient which projected into our lines. Here we have a more or less straight front, except on our right flank at Verdun, which is refused or sloped back and to the right.

This gives an excellent opportunity for the German Aviation to attack us in flank in the air. This nearly always leads to a rear attack. It is even more serious in the air than is a similar attack on the ground. During the Battle of Verdun in August, 1917, I saw the German Aviation come in from the right of the Verdun and shoot down the French balloons without mercy, and also cover the French lines with their reconnaissance planes everywhere.

I know that this same thing would happen to us when once the battle starts. Therefore, as far as enemy reconnaissance and work over our own ground troops by German planes is concerned, I have to watch our right flank. In St. Mihiel, on account of the shape of the front, I had an opportunity to send heavy masses of the air force into one side of the salient, then into the other side, keeping the enemy constantly occupied.

Here, being unable to do this, I have decided to mass our offensive aviation on the main axis of liaison, or the center axis of advance of the whole army. This line runs from Epinonville to Romagne to Banthéville. This is the area through which the highroads that supply the German army come from the north.

Our object in doing this is to destroy the German stores of ammunition and supplies in the area behind the army, to attack any infantry reserves coming up, and also to force the air fighting well into German territory.

I think that the time has come, as our air reenforcements are rapidly moving up, when we can push the fighting farther and farther into the enemy's country. From an air standpoint, the two important places on our flanks are Dun-sur-Meuse on the Meuse River on the right, and Grand Pré on the edge of the Argonne Forest, and the roads north of it, on our left.

PART SIX

Sept., 1918 (Continued).

OUR whole front on the ground is about fifty miles long. Our straight-line distance in the air, however, is a little over thirty miles from one side to the other. This is a tremendous battle front, however, for a single attack.

Our Army has ready to put into the line more than half a million troops and 4,200 pieces of artillery—the greatest mass of artillery ever brought together under one single direction for a battle.

The ground in front of us is very bad, chopped up with hills, woods, brush, and streams. The French have been able to make virtually no headway against the Germans in this area since the beginning of the war. The Germans have it remarkably well organized, with trenches and machine-gun nests. They have always held this part of the front with comparatively few men, so as to release more men for operations elsewhere.

In addition to our own aviation, I am getting considerable assistance from the French, two Italian bombardment squadrons, and General Trenchard, whose British Independent Air Force cooperates with us in bombarding the German airdromes and supply points.

General Pershing decided that the initial attack should

take place on September 26. Accordingly, I assembled the officers of the various aviation units in the afternoon of September 24, to give them their instructions.

I had previously asked General Pershing if he would come up to meet the air officers when they were assembled, and he told me that he would be very glad to. I went down to his headquarters to get him, and he immediately dropped the work he was doing and accompanied me with his aide, Major Bowditch, up the little street of Souilly. I had given instructions that the automobiles and motorcycles of the visiting officers should be carefully concealed from overhead view, knowing that a hostile airplane might come over us, take photographs, and thereby disclose our position.

We arrived at my headquarters, where the foreign officers and our own were now assembled for orders. General Pershing gave them a very nice talk and told them how much he appreciated the work we had done at St. Mihiel and that he relied on the Air Service to be the eyes of the Army and to lead us forward to victory again in the Argonne. I walked back with him to his headquarters and then quickly returned to my own.

I had hardly sat down before Colonel Dodd, my information officer, came in with a report that a German Rumpler two-seater airplane had been detected crossing from the direction of Verdun toward the northwest, 21,000 feet up, and had been shot down in our own territory by a patrol from the First Pursuit Group

Some of the plates had been captured intact and were being developed. This was the airplane that had passed over us when I brought General Pershing up. The development of the plates revealed a perfect picture of Souilly, with the motor cars grouped around my headquarters.

Our attack was launched in the early morning of September 26. The artillery bombardment was terrific. How much good it did I do not know—I don't think very much. I had put a small advance airdrome just outside of Verdun, which was only about three and one-half miles from the front lines, and had placed a flight of planes there to be constantly on the alert to attack any German low flying planes that came in opposite our right flank. It was commanded by Lieutenant Vasconcelles.

When the artillery preparation opened in the early morning, the cannonade was so terrific and the reverberation in the air was so great that the metal gasoline tanks on the Spad airplanes of Vasconcelles' flight were sprung and made to leak.

There was a little mist on the morning of September 26, but the rest of the day proved fair and rather warmer than the day before. The visibility was quite good. Our airplanes left the ground before the break of day and were well out on the German side when the battle got in full swing.

Again we dominated the air, but not to the extent that we had at St. Mihiel. Not only had the Germans more airplanes in the vicinity, but the shape of the front was such that it was extremely difficult to keep the German planes out from one flank or the other.

Our bombardment aviation, acting well into the enemy's country, kept them pretty busy and, although many incursions were made on our side of the line, we kept the air fighting, generally speaking, well away from our ground troops.

Late in the afternoon of the day of the attack, when flying over the central part of our line, I noticed a terrible congestion of motor traffic at Avocourt.

Columns of our transportation stood several miles long on three roads running into Avocourt, where they all came together. Not a wheel could be turned, either to the front or to the rear, because the trucks were in no man's land and if they did not stick to the roads they would immediately mire down for good.

If the German Aviation had been able to attack this column, it certainly would have destroyed it. This would have put the whole central army corps, the Fifth, out of ammunition and supplies. A counterattack then by a small organization of Germans would have broken a hole right straight through the center of our line, and nothing could have stopped it, because we could not have moved troops up along the roads to help the Fifth Corps.

We had received many reports that the German Aviation had received armored airplanes that could resist machine-gun fire with which to attack our organizations on the front. Here in this great congestion of motor trucks was the target for which they had been waiting.

I immediately concentrated all our bombardment aviation

against Romagne and Dun-sur-Meuse, so as to keep the fighting in the back areas and make the German pursuit aviation remain twenty or thirty kilometers away from the line to defend these important places.

I assigned the First Pursuit Group under Hartney to keep up a constant patrol at an altitude of only about 300 feet—in fact, almost down among the infantry—so as to prevent the hostile airplanes from getting in there. Had we not done this instantly, I believe that this whole mass of transportation would have been destroyed and burned up by the German Air Service.

As we were pushing in the air so strongly, fifteen or twenty miles the other side of the infantry, the Germans could send no pursuit airplanes with their battle flights to protect them. The result was that our pursuit airplanes shot down great numbers of the enemy's attack aviation which was attempting to destroy our truck trains.

Reports came in from the front lines at this time that the German aviators kept constantly over them and that our planes would not attack them; so I sent Colonel Dodd up there on the ground. He went as far as he could in a motor-cycle, and then got out and walked for miles around the stalled transport. He reported to me that all the trucks of three divisions had been routed through the one center of Avocourt, and that it would take three days for the engineers to make roads for them to move away.

Dodd also reported that he saw no German aircraft over our front at low altitude, and that he observed six combats on the enemy's side of the line. He met the general of our forces who had complained that German airplanes were constantly near them. When Dodd asked him how he knew they were German airplanes, he replied, "When we fire machine guns at them they retire into Germany"—that is, on the German side of the line.

As a matter of fact, they were the airplanes of Hartney's pursuit group, flying low and watching every part of the line to guard against the low flying enemy attack, and our troops not only did not know them, but kept shooting at them.

The Germans have painted their airplanes so that they look just like the ground when seen from above. The German airmen get down to within one hundred feet or so of the earth, or even lower at times, fly up ravines or behind forests, and pounce on infantry columns or wagon trains, surprising them before they can conceal themselves.

We had a couple of engineer companies lined up for mess that were attacked in this way by a flight of German attack aviation. They killed eighty-seven men and wounded a couple of hundred before the engineers could get to cover.

Fortunately, by the last day of the month this terrible mess of motor trucks in the center of our line was straightened out. The commanding general of the corps was relieved and another one put in command of it.

Our troops kept attacking the German position and getting terrific losses from a comparatively small number of Germans, in proportion to the ground that we gained. All of the ground in front of the German position was very well organized and defended by German machine-gun troops, excellently trained and well protected.

The Argonne Battle was not a particularly interesting one from an air standpoint. The infantry on the ground just knocked its head against a stone wall. It was terrible for us to look down from the air and see the uncoordinated, not to say disorganized, nature of the combat which resulted from not using the airplanes for reconnaissance sufficiently.

At one place infantry attacked all alone without artillery helping them. A little way off an entirely separate combat was taking place; then again a little farther on there was no fighting. In another place the artillery was firing with terrific speed against nothing, and the infantry was waiting word to occupy the ground supposed to be held by the enemy when really there was no enemy within a long way of it.

The troops nearly always completely lose contact with the enemy. Then when they do come up they are surprised by the German machine-gun nests in prepared positions and suffer terrific casualties.

There is one thing to be said, however, and that is, in spite of the losses, General Pershing has never faltered in pushing the offensive.

Our pilots have to fly right down and almost shake hands with the infantry on the ground to find out where they are. Many of the infantry and artillery officers leave the handling of the wireless stations to the first sergeants. The sergeants say that they get tired of seeing wireless operators sitting in a hole in the ground, safe from the enemy's fire, doing nothing as they suppose, and assign them to kitchen police or some other duty of that kind.

As a result there are no communications at a critical time. It is practically impossible to impress the men in the ranks, through their own officers, as to the value of aviation. They do not even know what the insignia on our planes is in many cases.

I have had Colonel Dodd prepare the following which we throw down from our airplanes to all the infantry positions:

FROM THE AMERICAN SCRAPPERS IN THE AIR TO AMERICAN SCRAPPERS ON THE GROUND

DOUGHBOYS:

While you are giving the Boche hell on the ground, we are helping you to the limit in the air.

The artillery is behind you, anxious to help with their shells.

Headquarters is trying through us to keep in close touch with you and to render aid whenever you are checked or outnumbered.

Keep us posted at all times as to where your front lines are, either with Bengal lights, panels, or—if nothing else is available—wave a white towel or any white cloth.

Your signals enable us:

To take news of your location to the rear.

To report if the attack is successful.

To call for help if needed.

To enable the artillery to put their shells over your head into the enemy.

We prevent the enemy planes from telling the enemy artillery where you are; we bomb and machine-gun enemy troops whenever the chance offers.

If you are out of ammunition and tell us, we will report it and have it sent up.

If you are surrounded, we will deliver the ammunition by airplane.

We do not hike through the mud with you, but

there are discomforts in our work as bad as mud. We won't let rain, storms, Archies, nor Boche planes prevent our getting there with the goods.

Do not think that we are not on the job when you cannot see us—most of our planes work so far in front that they cannot be seen from the lines.

Some enemy planes may break through our airplane barrage in front of you, and may sometimes bomb and machine-gun you, but in the last month we have dropped ten tons of bombs for every one the Boche has dropped. For every Boche plane that you see over you, the Boche sees ten Allied planes over him. For every balloon that he burns, we burn eight.

Our losses of aviators correspond to your losses; but for every one that we lose the Boche has to pay with heavy interest.

Whenever a Boche plane is brought down in your sector, do not collect souvenirs from it; you may remove an article or marking that would give valuable information to us. If Boche aviators are not dead when they land, wait ten minutes before approaching within one hundred feet of the plane after they have left it; sometimes they start a bomb. *Do not touch anything in a Boche plane*—they sometimes carry innocent looking infernal machines.

Use us to the limit, show your panels, burn the signal lights, wave a cloth; anything to tell us where you are and what you need.

After reading this, pass it on to your Buddie, and— remember to show your signals.

YOUR AVIATOR.

October, 1918.

A good many visitors came up during October. Colonel Arthur Woods of New York visited me and I took him up for a flight over the front. John T. McCutcheon of Chicago, the eminent cartoonist and writer, I took up also. Mr. John D. Ryan, the Assistant Secretary of War in charge of Aviation, was also here.

We had a conference in my battle headquarters in Souilly at which I explained the situation of the air forces in Europe to Mr. Ryan. He seemed to understand what was going on better than any other of the department heads I have seen.

Our air fighting is continuous and of a very intense character. The morale of our men in the air has kept going up all of the time in spite of their heavy losses, as they feel more and more that the tide of victory is dependent on air supremacy if the war lasts much longer. On the ground I believe that the morale of the men is going down, due to the terrific losses.

Some rather foolish orders have been issued from the headquarters of the First Army. These orders directed that attacks be made on positions that are really impregnable against the means that we have of advancing. Our forces would be ordered to advance eight or ten kilometers, whereas all the fighting troops on the front know that it is impossible to advance more than two or three kilometers without bringing up supplies and supports.

Many of them consequently did not try to comply with the orders, knowing full well that they could not execute them without getting away out of supporting distance of the troops on each side of them. The result is that our line is not uniform in any way.

The organization of our Second American Army is now being pushed. This army is to be located in the Toul area, to act on the right of the First American Army and to attack the great city of Metz, fortified by the Germans to the limit of their ability.

It was therefore decided that we should assign a certain amount of aviation to each army and then assemble all of the pursuit and bombardment aviation that we could and mass it into a great force with which to strike deep into Germany.

General Pershing informed me that I would command the whole air force; that is, the aviation of both the armies and in addition the general reserve of aviation which would be assigned to the group of armies.

General Pershing is to give up the command of the First Army and turn it over to General Liggett. Then he will assume command of the group of armies as soon as the Second Army becomes capable of functioning. General Bullard is to assume command of the Second Army.

The days wear on with constant hammering by the infantry against the German positions. The flying in support of the

First Army has become more or less routine matter. There was one day, however, October 9, when the enemy had assembled a considerable force of infantry and artillery on the east bank of the Meuse, opposite the right flank of our Third Corps, commanded by General Bullard.

These German troops were being concentrated in the woods near a place called Damvillers. If they could creep in against our right flank and make a surprise attack, they would cause a great deal of damage. If we could smash up their concentration, blow up their ammunition dumps, and burn their supplies by an attack from the air, the whole German maneuver might be stopped.

Accordingly I asked the French Air Division if they could assist me in such an operation. They replied immediately by sending 322 airplanes in a single formation carrying thirty-nine tons of bombs to attack this place.

Our Aviation redoubled its efforts along the front of our troops and against the German supply points that we had been attacking before.

The great air formation flew right over our whole army on this beautiful clear day. I had to act so quickly that I had no time to inform General Pershing or the staff of this attack; so when it approached I ran over to the General's headquarters and showed him and his staff officers this marvelous picture as the airplanes passed over. I then went back to the airdrome and got in my airplane to see the effect of the air attack against Damvillers, and also to look over the position of our own air forces along our front.

The French had thrown down thirty-nine tons of bombs on the Damvillers area, causing numerous fires and the destruction of some of the roads and railways in that vicinity. They blew up several ammunition dumps, hit a troop concentration in a wood, and caused heavy losses to the Germans.

They had numberous air combats with the Germans, as a result of which they shot down twelve German airplanes in flames and returned to our side of the line without the loss of a single ship.

A view of this attack is impossible to describe. Squadron after squadron of Bréguet bombers flying in V formation at about 12,000 feet went straight to their objective. On each side of them and above and below hovered small single-seater airplanes for their protection.

As they arrived over the target the leading squadron of from fifteen to eighteen airplanes dropped all of its bombs at once. As each airplane carried about ten bombs, this meant 150 bombs to each discharge. As the bombs struck the ground terrific explosions and detonations took place which we could easily hear up in the air. Within a minute after the first squadron attacked, the second one attacked, and so on until twelve squadrons had delivered their bombs.

While this was going on, sixty German pursuit planes were attempting in every way to get at the bombers. They came down from the direction of the sun in a succession of groups of from ten to fifteen airplanes each; the French pursuit aviation handled them beautifully. Whenever they came within reach they were set upon by about three French airplanes to one of the Germans'.

Individual combats were taking place all around the bombardment ships, above, below, and on each side of them, but not one bombardment plane was shot down, nor was a pursuit plane lost on the enemy side of the lines; whereas we received official credit for twelve enemy planes shot down.

During the night of October 9 the British Aviation threw down forty-two tons of bombs, which gave a grand total of eighty-one tons of bombs thrown down within twenty-four hours on the enemy's side of the line.

All of this hammering was having a great effect on the Germans. Reports were coming in from prisoners which showed that we were destroying numbers of their airplanes and making such holes in their airdromes that they constantly had to make new ones. After each of our attacks the German machines returning at night would find holes big enough to smash their planes directly in the middle of their supposedly good flying fields.

One day I wandered into General Bullard's headquarters. He was very busy, as usual. I explained to him that his troops were not using their air service sufficiently: that the artillery would not ask for an airplane before they began a certain shoot, but would wait until after they got into position and be ready to shoot, and then would think an airplane ought to appear by divine providence. General Bullard called in his aide and directed him to send out a very strong message on this subject to all commanders.

My old friend General Brewster, the Inspector General, was present, and was chuckling at our conversation. At the end of it General Bullard said, "Mitchell, there is an enemy balloon right opposite me which sees everything we are doing and I wish you would shoot it down." I replied that I would do so at once.

As a matter of fact, I already had ordered an attack on this balloon some hours before and I knew that the airplanes would be there within a few minutes. I called up the First Pursuit Group and asked Hartney when the attack would begin and he said that they were about to start.

An attack against a balloon requires considerable preparation and cannot be done on the spur of the moment. The balloon has to be located, has to be approached from different directions, several feints have to be made so as to draw off the hostile pursuit aviation, and then the main attack is launched from an unexpected direction so as to surprise them.

I did not tell General Bullard about these preparations, but I did tell him to watch in the direction of the balloon in about one-half hour and he would see a big column of smoke appear. I left his headquarters, and had hardly gone back a mile along the road when over us came the flights of the First Pursuit Group on the balloon mission. Within a few minutes afterward the German balloon was in flames and a great column of smoke was ascending into the sky.

I had hardly reached my headquarters when General Bullard called me up and congratulated me. I told my staff and the First Pursuit Group about what had happened and we laughed heartily about it. General Bullard to this day thinks that we organized the attack and shot down the balloon after he requested it.

A day or two after this, Martin Egan, the veteran newspaper correspondent, came to my headquarters, and I took him around with me to the various pursuit and bombardment groups as I inspected them. I am always glad to take men of his caliber with me. He has great breadth of view and not only observes things but reasons out what it is all about.

It is strange how very few officers of the ground army

ever come near our airdromes. Even the chiefs of staff
and commanding generals are seldom seen upon them. When
they do come they know almost nothing about them and do

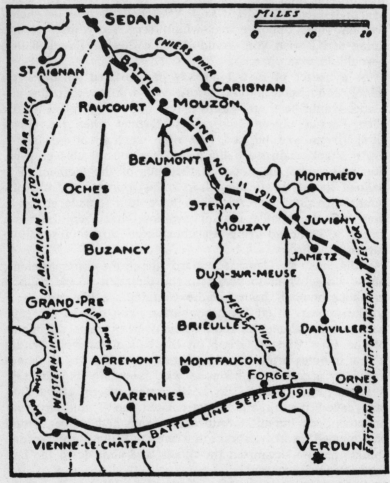

*Map shows the Meuse-Argonne battle fronts September 26
to November 11, 1918. The dotted line shows the ground
gained by the A. E. F. in its greatest battle of the World
War.*

not seem to want to learn. The whole flying game is so far
beyond them that they know it is impossible for them to
learn it, and therefore attempt to hide their ignorance by a

lot of bombastic talk and bluff to cover it up.

I had a long conference with General Pershing on October 17. We discussed the formation of aviation for the group of armies. I also proposed to him that in the spring of 1919, when I would have a great force of bombardment airplanes, he assign one of the infantry divisions permanently to the Air Service, preferably the First Division; that we arm the men with a great number of machine guns and train them to go over the front in our large airplanes, which would carry ten or fifteen of these soldiers each.

We could equip each man with a parachute, so that when we desired to make a rear attack on the enemy we could carry these men over the lines and drop them off in parachutes behind the German position. They could assemble at a prearranged strong point and fortify it. We could supply them by aircraft with food and ammunition.

Our low flying attack aviation would then cover every road in their vicinity, both day and night, so as to prevent the Germans falling on them until they could thoroughly organize the position.

Then we could attack the Germans from the rear, aided by an attack from our army on the front, and support the whole maneuver with our great air force.

Tanks have proved themselves to be the instrument par excellence in advancing over the ground, and I want to see just as great a development of this arm by the army as it is possible to make.

If we can get well to the rear of the enemy with our air forces and have tanks jump on them in front, we will come pretty near to destroying the German Army.

One of the battalions of the Seventy-seventh Division became detached from it and was surrounded by Germans in the Argonne Forest. It was commanded by Major Whittlesey. I ordered chocolate and concentrated food and ammunition dropped off to it. Our pilots thought they had located it from the panels that it showed, and they dropped off considerable supplies.

The battalion held out and rejoined its command, but I found that they had received none of the supplies we had dropped off, but that the Germans had made up a panel like theirs and our men had calmly dropped off the food to the Germans.

PART SEVEN

October—November, 1918.

HUNDREDS of combats in the air, the attack of German ground troops and the bombardment of enemy objectives, occur daily. It would take volumes to write about them. The results of these are contained in our daily operation reports.

One day our bombardment fliers attacked the railroad station at Longuyon. They missed the station by two and one-half miles, but hit in the middle of a German division at drill, killing and wounding over 2,000 men, including some of the members of the commanding general's staff.

Another night our bombardment aviation hit an ammunition train drawn up in the railroad station at Longuyon. On one side of it was an incoming train filled with troops, and on the other was a railroad train of men on leave going to the rear. About 500 men were killed outright and over 2,000 wounded.

One of our pilots put a bomb straight through the top of the roundhouse at Longuyon, destroying eight or ten locomotives in it, and blew up the whole place.

We have lost many a good man, and of course will continue to lose more. Many of these have been taken prisoners, and as our aviators know so much more about the general situation and the position of all the troops than any other officers of corresponding rank, we have to be very careful to instruct them as to what to do in case they are captured. The following is a list of dont's each aviator is supposed to know:

DONT'S FOR FLYERS WHO LAND IN ENEMY TERRITORY

It is important to impress upon pilots and observers, and any others whose duty may take them in an airplane across the lines, the following points with regard to minimizing the amount of information which the enemy would be able to obtain should the machine and occupants fall into their hands:

(1) Don't carry any papers, official or private, while in an airplane. Envelopes containing private correspondence give away the identification of the prisoner's unit.

(2) Don't mark airdromes and other information concerning our own side of the line on maps which are taken up into the air. The smallest mark is sufficient to indicate an airdrome to the enemy should the map be captured.

(3) Don't, if captured, trust anyone, whether in German uniform or uniform of any of the Allies. Speak as little as possible and don't enter into conversation. Friendliness shown by the enemy should at once cause suspicion.

(4) Don't forget that a clever interrogator will obtain information from you in the course of a casual conversation; therefore speak as little as possible.

(5) Don't address letters which the enemy says he will drop for you across the lines to your squadron wing or brigade. Address letters to the headquarters of your Air Service and they will be sent from there to their right destination.

(6) Don't forget that the Germans want to know, not only about aviation in general, but more particularly American aviation. They will make unrelenting efforts to obtain this.

(7) The Germans use listening apparatus in prisoner-of-war cages and other places where prisoners are located, so that conversation with other prisoners is overheard. Therefore don't discuss military or aviation matters of any sort or description with anyone, even your best friend, as your conversation will be overheard by the enemy.

(8) German interrogators will dress up as Allied officers or soldiers and will be placed in the same room as you, with the object of learning your information;

therefore again suspect anyone whom you do not actually know.

(9) Don't be misled by the kindness which will be shown to you when first captured. Champagne dinners and such things will be provided for you in order to get you to talk.

(10) Don't ever be put off your guard.

EXTRACT FROM THE STATEMENT OF AN OFFICER RECENTLY ESCAPED FROM GERMANY

I landed on a village green in the middle of a number of Germans. The Germans were all around the machine at once, and before I could realize where I was they were pulling me out of the plane. They did not treat me roughly. There were several German officers present.

I was taken to headquarters in the village, where I was interviewed by a general. I refused to give any information. After threatening me a little, the General retired. A German Flying Corps car came up and I was taken to an airdrome several miles back, where I was given lunch. The food was poor, but we had champagne.

Eight or ten German officers had lunch with me. They were very polite. They asked me a good many leading questions, but they got nothing out of me.

I was then taken to divisional (or corps) headquarters, where I was questioned by several officers. They were fairly polite. They seemed to know about most of the infantry battalions in that part of the line, where they were, the name of the C.O., and other particulars. They told me the position the battalion had occupied at Loos. It was all correct. They asked me for the position of General Headquarters, which they admitted they did not know.

I was then taken in the car to Cambrai, where I was placed in the Citadel. Here there were about 100 British soldiers with two officers besides myself (I am not sure of their regiment, but I think it was the Durham Light Infantry in the new army).

I was taken before Lieutenant Schram. He was very polite and asked me many questions as to the aërial

work, especially as to the Spad machine. He told me that
they had recently got some very useful information from
papers in a machine which had been shot down, which
contained instructions as to cooperation between the
air service and the infantry. He also asked me about
the tanks.

He also asked me many questions about two leading
men on our side whose names I do not remember,
though they were both knights. I cannot remember if
they were general officers or what their position was.
He wanted to get to know anything about them and
their movements and where they were. He was very
urgent about this.

WARNING TO BRITISH AVIATORS

*The following instructions in the form of a warning have
been given to British aviators. American officers and aviators
should note them and appreciate their importance:*

If you are unfortunate enough to be compelled to
land behind the German lines, you may be agreeably
surprised by the apparent hospitality and generosity of
your welcome there. The German officers will probably have you to stay with them as their guest for a
few days at one of their squadrons, and will make you
most comfortable.

You will probably be extremely well entertained with
the very best of everything they can offer. An abundance
of good champagne from France will oil the wheels
of conversation between the officers of the German Flying Corps and one whom they will probably term a
brother officer of the English Flying Corps. They will
appear to be very good fellows, straightforward, cheer-
ful, and will keep on the scientific side of flying, apart
from their ordinary work, with which they may say
you are quite fed up.

They will probably lead you to talk about the pos-
sibilities of aviation after the war, and profess little interest in aviation as actually applied to war. It may not
take much wine to gladden your heart and to induce

you to lay aside your suspicions and reserve and forget the guile which lies behind their artless questions.

And so, unaccustomed as you are to this form of
deceit, you may fall another victim to this clever combination of cunning and hospitality. But, though they
may succeed for the moment in making a favorable
impression, you will afterwards have every reason to remember that during this war the Germans have proved
themselves to be a cruel and unscrupulous enemy.

They are sound financiers and have an eye to good
investment. It does not cost them much to entertain
you well, and even if it did, they expect to get an ade-
quate return for their money in the form of information
unwittingly imparted by you.

That is why they give you all the delights of the
Carlton and Savoy, with none of the regrets of an over-
draft at Cox's, and that is why you will be treated as
a highly honored guest instead of being half starved
in one of their now notorious prison camps, a treatment
which is in fact only postponed until they have squeezed
every ounce of useful information out of you.

The work is done by experienced men. Quite unknown
to yourself, one or more of the seemingly irresponsible
flying men are highly trained intelligence officers who
will sift bits of useful information from your most
brilliant *bon mot*.

On the other hand, different methods may be employed, though these are not so common with prisoners
of the Flying Corps as with others. You may be brow-
beaten and ordered to disclose information under pain
of suffering severe penalties if you refuse. Remember
that this is only a ruse and that they will not carry
out their threats.

It is quite possible that you may be placed in a hut
with an officer alleged to be an English prisoner, speaking English fluently, knowing many people in England
well, and wishing to have news of everyone and everything. Perhaps he will ask no questions, relying only on
your confidence. It will be difficult for you to believe
that he is not a companion in misfortune.

Therefore be on your guard and remember that in a

show like this it is impossible for any individual not at the head of affairs to say what is of use to the enemy and what is not.

Remember that any information you may inadvertently give may lengthen the war and keep you longer in Germany; may cost the lives of many Englishmen; may strain the country's resources even more than they are being strained at present.

Don't think this is all imagination and needless caution. The need of it has been brought out by experience.

We continue, of course, to receive many complaints from the ground troops about not getting enough airplanes to them, and that the observers don't see them nor repeat their signals at the time that they are required. Our airmen stay on the line all of the time, whereas the troops on the ground are changed frequently. The result is, comparatively speaking, that the men in the air are much more familiar with their particular duties than those on the ground.

It now remains for us to assemble a great force of bombardment and pursuit planes with which to attack the interior of Germany. If the war lasts, I am sure that air power will decide it. I laid out the program for doing this and set my staff to selecting the points where these new units equipped with the Handley-Page and Caproni bombardment airplanes, combined with DHs, built in the United States, would be placed.

We also figured out how they were to operate in combination with the British and the French. There is considerable talk now of combining all the aviation under one command. The English command the sea forces, with Admiral Beatty as the head. The French command the armies on the land, with General Foch at the head. It is proposed that America be assigned the aviation, and that I command it.

November, 1918.

There is a good deal of talk that General Pershing is to be relieved of command of the A.E.F., presumably on account of the losses that we are incurring in the Argonne.

There is a rumor that General March, the Chief of Staff in the United States, may replace him.

In this kind of war if attacks are to be pushed it is impossible to avoid losses. The day of grand maneuvers, flanking attacks, and enveloping and surrounding an enemy on the ground is practically a thing of the past. The old professional armies have led us into this method of war, which is merely a contest of exhaustion. We Americans ought to be able to last longer than the others can, but of course we shall have to pay dearly in lives.

General Pershing is playing the game, and playing it as well as he can; and now that we really have a great American Army in operation, it would be a shame to change commanders, with all the troubles and mix-ups which would ensue. We have had a good test of what changes every little while mean in aviation, which set us back months.

Our air attacks against the German airdromes, supply points, and communications have begun to have a decided effect. The German citizens have been complaining to their government and becoming more insistent that they be given protection.

Winter is now facing us; but with its coming we hear that the Germans are weakening and that the interior of Germany is becoming more and more a prey to a revolutionary movement.

As the time for the Armistice approached and it became known that it meant the end of the war, the nervous tension to which all had been subjected began to let up. In the Air Service, where certain German air pilots were known individually by the markings on their planes, and who in turn recognized our men, the pilots went out for one last fight.

Very much in the same way that the knights used to do in the days gone by, they challenged the opposing aviators for individual combats by flying around the hostile airdromes. I believe that the last German shot down by an American aviator was the victory which Major Maxwell Kirby gained over his adversary on the morning of November 11.

No people knew better than those in the Air Service what a continuation of the war meant. We had all preparations complete to carry the war into the heart of Germany in the spring of 1919.

The air weapons that would have been used would have caused untold suffering. Chemical weapons most certainly would have been brought into play—gases for destroying cattle and sheep, and incendiary projectiles for burning the crops and forests.

During a war of this kind one's nerves, passions, and whole physical and mental make-up are tremendously over-wrought and one's outlook is somewhat different than it would be ordinarily.

During the last six months of the war I doubt if I actually slept more than three hours a day. This was because the reports of the day's activities along our front did not reach my headquarters until about ten o'clock at night. They would then be arranged by the appropriate staff section and I would begin their complete perusal somewhere around midnight. I would then dictate the orders for the following day and carefully check their proper sending to every unit.

It would be two o'clock by that time, and I would be up at five so as to watch the action of our forces that took the air before daylight.

When the order came to cease hostilities I realized that I was pretty tired and that everyone around me was very much the same way. I was glad to see the terriffic loss of life being stopped, because with our green and untrained troops we were losing a great many more men than were our Allies.

Of course it was to be expected that the Europeans would not allow us to reap any more of the fruits of victory than was possible.

While on the one hand we had unquestionably won the war for the Allies—as they would certainly have been defeated by Germany without our entrance—on the other hand, it was their fight and they had put up the greatest sacrifices.

We also were fighting to keep the advantages in commerce and finance which we had gained as a result of the war. The Germans certainly were not destroyed, or hardly defeated. They were repulsed and thrown back; but their troops would have continued to fight bravely on the line if the interior of Germany had not gone to pieces behind them. We hear that the Kaiser and the court have fled to Holland and that the whole country is a prey to revolution.

So now the Germans are retreating. But they have done all the fighting on foreign soil. The only damage that has come to their own country has been through the air. The Allies have paid dearly for everything they have obtained, because, according to the present system of war, ground armies are incapable of inflicting a decisive defeat in a short time on an adversary.

The evening of November 10 I went from my headquarters at Ligny to Toul, where I found the staff of the Second Army preparing an attack for the following day. This, it seemed to me, was a rather foolish proceeding, as it would lead to no benefit to us and would kill a great many men, because the Germans would certainly resist them. The division to be used was the Ninety-second, composed of colored troops, who had had very little experience on the front.

This attack was actually carried out the following morning, with disastrous results.

As I went back to my headquarters late at night, I could see ammunition dumps exploding on the German side, rockets being fired in the air, and rejoicing going on wherever it was possible on the French side. Some could hardly understand that peace was at hand.

A few of the peasants I talked to were very skeptical. The poor things had been at it for over four years, and their minds had become so fixed with the idea of war that it would take some time to unfix them.

The morning of November 11 I visited the commanding officers of the Air Service of both armies that were under me and congratulated them on the great work they had done. This was the first time in the world's history that great bodies of air troops had been brought together and fought as a single organization.

We Americans had developed the best system of air fighting that the world had ever seen. We had entered into full combat with the splendid air troops that the Germans had trained for over three years of war before we joined. We not only held our own, but greatly excelled it. We could look with absolute confidence to the future if our system were maintained and our men who were trained in actual combat were given charge of the development to make America absolutely safe from hostile invasion.

The day has passed when armies on the ground or navies on the sea can be the arbiter of a nation's destiny in war. The main power of defense and the power of initiative against an enemy has passed to the air.

My reports on the morning of November 11 showed that I had present on the front in the hands of American units 740 airplanes. Of these, 528 were of French manufacture, 16 were of British manufacture, and 196 were of American manufacture.

Just think—one year and eight months after the war began the United States had only been able to put 196 airplanes on the front! We did practically all our fighting with foreign machines. There was no excuse for this whatever.

My figures show that from the time that American air units entered into combat on the front—that is, from March, 1918, to November 11, 1918—our men shot down and received official confirmation for 927 enemy airplanes or balloons. During the same time we lost, due to operations of the enemy, 316 of our airplanes or balloons.

This ratio of three to one was a most remarkable thing and was much greater in proportion than the victories achieved by any of our Allies. The reason was that we had remarkable pilots and that our tactics and strategy were superior to any of those employed elsewhere.

Everyone was rejoicing. After giving the necessary instructions to have every organization write up its war experiences, I decided to take a trip into Paris to see what was going on in the French capital.

I took my largest automobile and gathered up some of my friends, who had been so kind to us during the war, and proceeded to the capital. Everyone was trying to get to Paris that could. The roads were choked with automobiles.

We reached there quite late in the evening, and found the Champs Elysées in a great uproar.

Men and women were pulling captured German cannon, which had lined the street, up and down the pavements. Girls were dressed in soldiers' caps and blouses and going

through the drill around the guns that the artillerymen
were taught on the front. Everyone was singing, shaking
hands, kissing each other, dancing, screaming, and yell-
ing—the most spectacular outburst of feeling that I have
ever seen.

The people had been almost sure that they would be defeated in some way or other before the war was over, and
now they had actually obtained victory! How great it was,
no one could tell; but they were victorious, and their joy
knew no bounds.

They were very open in what they said about the Americans that night. Everywhere that an American soldier was
seen he was hailed as a hero and a deliverer. It was funny
how quickly a French soldier could tell whether he had
been serving on the front or in the interior.

We got a little supper, then started down in my automobile to the boulevards. Everywhere people were jumping
on the running boards and embracing the chauffeur and
mechanic who were driving my car. The streets surged with
the populace and none but military cars were allowed to
proceed. When we arrived at the boulevards it was nearly
midnight, and a never to be forgotten sight presented itself.

People in all sorts of costumes—singing, shouting, yell-
ing, crying, some of them fighting, and acting all sorts of
ways—were there. A cordon of police closed the boulevards to all vehicles; but, as a gendarme was telling my
chauffeur that the street was closed, we were recognized
by a crowd of pilots of the French Air Division who had
served under me at the attack of St. Mihiel and in the
Argonne. These screamed, *"Vive notre Général Améri-
cain!"* and, throwing the gendarme to one side, they almost
picked up the automobile and carried it right down the
boulevards.

I counted eighteen of them sitting on the roof, on the
radiator, on the mud guards, and all over the back. They
formed a ring hand in hand around the car, both men
and women, singing the Marseillaise and Madelon and some
of the aviators' songs, and literally carried us from one
end of the boulevards to the other. We were in the only automobile, I believe, that was on the boulevards that night.
It was a great experience.

The map shows the various engagements of the A. E. F. and
the divisions taking part: (A) Ypres-Lys, August 19-November
11; 27, 30, 37, and 91 divisions. (B) Somme, August 8-
November 11; 27, 30, and 33 divisions. (C) Aisne-Marne,
July 18-August 6; 1, 2, 3, 4, 26, 28, 32, and 42 divisions.
(D) Oise-Aisne, August 18-November 11; 28, 32, and 77
divisions. (E) Meuse-Argonne, September 20-November 11;
1, 2, 3, 4, 5, 26, 28, 29, 32, 33, 35, 37, 42, 77, 78, 79, 80,
82, 89, 90, and 91 divisions. (F) St. Mihiel, September 12-16;
1, 2, 4, 5, 26, 42, 82, 89, and 90 divisions.

The following day and night there was very much the
same celebration.

The following day I worked in the Paris office and saw
General McAndrew, our Chief of Staff Harbord, and Dun-

woody. On November 14 I went to Chaumont and had a good talk with General Pershing. He told me he wanted me to take the Air Service up to the Rhine with the Third American Army, which was being organized to occupy the territory up there in accordance with the treaty.

Only the oldest units in the Air Service were to go. These were to be filled up to their full strength with pilots, mechanics, and men. Likewise, the ground troops were to have the oldest and best organizations. General Dickman is to command the army. He had distinguished himself in all the fighting. He is of German extraction and speaks German with great fluency.

It is strange how many Germans we have that have distinguished themselves in our service, and what efficient officers and patriotic Americans they are. Of course it is not strange, because we are made up of the nations of northern Europe, and all of the countries in northern Europe have a large Germanic element in them, even the French.

On November 14 an order was issued placing me in command of the air troops to go to the Rhine. All the other troops now were given a schedule of training which would keep them busy until they could be sent back to the United States.

We began to liquidate all our establishments and to turn in, store, or sell all our property, keeping, of course a sufficient amount ready in case there was any interference with the Armistice.

I returned to my headquarters at Ligny and reorganized my staff for the advance into Germany. From November 14 until November 17 I visited the various organizations that had been under my command, including the British, the French, and the Italian.

I never imagined that allies belonging to different nations could work together the way we did in the Air Force. It is impossible with ground troops. With us in the air we were all striving to perfect and develop a new power that the world has never seen before, which calls for qualities that are entirely different from those on the ground, and we therefore were all more or less on an even footing.

PART EIGHT

November, 1918 (continued).

MARSHALL FOCH had assembled a great force behind our Second Army just before the Armistice, consisting of the Moroccan Division and other French assault troops under General Mangin, for the purpose of delivering a great blow against Metz. The attack of our Second Army was a part of this general plan, which would been driven through about November 12 had the Armistice not come.

On November 17 I went to Longuyon, which formerly had been on the German side, with our leading troops. The enemy began to withdraw from our front immediately. They had left a great deal of artillery and many other things along the road. The country, however, looked very well policed by the Germans.

General von Gallwitz was in command of the group of German armies on our front. He was given only a week to withdraw his forces to the Rhine. This was a difficult thing to do under the conditions, because the whole organization of German territory had broken down behind him. A committee of soldiers, sailors, and workmen had taken charge of the various municipalities and local governments, displacing the regular constituted authorities.

Everywhere that we went there was constant evidence of how thoroughly the German Army had attempted to carry out its part of the Armistice agreement. Of course, everyone was short of food and our supply departments gave the people food wherever they needed it.

Great streams of prisoners were returning—British, French, and Russians—and they had many stories to tell. When the Armistice came, their prison camps were closed and they were told to shift for themselves. They sought assistance from the German Soldiers' Councils in the towns through which they passed, and were directed through Luxembourg and on toward Verdun. As a rule the people were kind to them.

December, 1918.

The weather is entirely different from that of a year ago. Then we were having heavy frost and snow, and great numbers of our men were sick and having a pretty sorry time of it. Now the weather is excellent. The men are stepping out along the roads into Germany, well equipped, gay and healthy. Our troops have continued the move to Coblenz and the Rhine by the way of Treves with great regularity and without hardships.

On December 2 I received a telegram announcing the death of Willard Straight in Paris. He was one of my lifelong friends and, had the war continued, was to join my staff.

On December 5, taking Colonel Paegelow with me, I went to Treves and looked over the airdrome. There is a large Zeppelin hangar at this place and in it the Germans had left 121 airplanes of all kinds. The German air officers were still there in command, and I arranged with them about sending our own officers up to take over the equipment.

I was driving my own machine, which was a German racing car. I had the chauffeur in a little rumble seat behind. The German officers asked if all the American generals drove their own cars. Paegelow answered that they did not, but as we had only one General in the Air Service, he had to get around very fast from place to place and that therefore I drove myself in order to do so.

A couple of days after this, while passing through Luxembourg, I met Senator "Jim" Wadsworth of New York and Arthur Page, who had come up on a rubbernecking expedition. I certainly was glad to see them. Page was getting data together for a book on the war, and Wadsworth was watching the political side of it as well as the military.

One would think that the commander of a victorious army such as this is would naturally be a candidate for the Presidency of one party or another after the war. I doubt very much, however, if General Pershing ever is.

I do not know that he wants to be, because the Commander of the American Expeditionary Forces is as high a position as any individual should ever desire.

The average man who has participated in this war thinks of the regular army professional soldier, and particularly a graduate of West Point, as being a "hard-boiled," heartless, and relentless disciplinarian, and practically nothing

The shaded portion of the map shows the section of Germany held by the American Army of Occupation.

else. There is a good deal to this, because the average regular army officer knows very little about the psychology of the masses, nor how the great body of his fellow men think and feel. He is brought up in a more or less narrow, machinelike atmosphere, which does not lead to the confidence of a great citizen army.

On December 8 I moved my headquarters to Treves and occupied the house of the Superintendent of Railways. He came in to call on me that evening. His principal conversation hinged around the fact that the Germans had been called Huns. He explained that they were accused of all sorts of atrocities merely for propaganda purposes.

Treves is an interesting old city. It was a garrison town of the Romans and contains many of the old Roman ruins, including an amphitheater. It is the headquarters for the hierarchy of the Roman Catholic Church in this part of the country and an archbishop resides here.

The Germans are very short of butter fats, lard, meat, soaps, and things of that kind. A great deal of their cloth has paper fiber woven into it.

From Treves I went to Coblenz. The last German troops had left. The crossing of the Rhine by these veterans was a serious occasion. The German soldiers formed in the street, with banners flying and their arms burnished. The muzzles of their rifles and the mouths of their cannons were decorated with flowers by the populace. They marched across the Rhine to the strains of their great national hymn, Die Wacht am Rhein, while the people wept.

Not for over a century has a hostile foot touched the soil of Germany north of the Rhine. During that time the German people have grown from a lot of little kingdoms and principalities to one of the mightiest nations that the world has ever seen.

One cannot help but think that Germany threw up the sponge pretty quickly during this war, compared to what he did in the past.

During the Thirty Years' War her people were reduced to nothing. They ate rats and anything they could get hold of. But during the last thirty or forty years the Germans have grown fat, rich, opulent, and pleasure loving.

It looks as if the moral fiber of this great people has been impaired to some extent by luxury and ease. The war has not yet been brought home to the masses of the German people, except to a small extent through the air. Of course they knew it was coming, but they hesitated to carry the war to a finish. Our President's Fourteen Points may have had a great deal to do with the Kaiser fleeing out of Germany, because he believed that if he stayed in Germany good terms in the treaty of peace could not possibly be obtained.

My old friend Colonel Jim Rhea is at Coblenz as the head of our Bridgehead Commission. He is to take over the bridges from the Germans. On the German side, Major von Sigel is in charge. He has with him his assistant, Lieutenant Schultze. Schultze was for many years a resident of Seattle, Washington; but, being a reserve officer when Germany entered the war he immediately went home to serve with the colors.

Schultze was the information officer of this division when they were opposite the Seventy-seventh New York Division when Whittlesey's battalion was lost. It was under Schultze's direction that the Germans put out the panels which were mistaken by our aviators for those of the lost battalion and caused them to drop so much food, chocolate, and cigarettes which the Germans immediately took and converted to their own uses.

Both von Sigel and Schultze said they knew when their attack at Château-Thierry was unsuccessful that the whole power of ending the war lay in the hands of the Americans. Up to that time they were certain that they would win. But the coming of the countless thousands of our men and the ever increasing number of aircraft and artillery on the front made them certain that, unless the great losses suffered by our armies caused the American people to pull our troops out of Europe, the Germans were surely gone.

Von Sigel helped me out very much in looking up airdromes for our squadrons. I mentioned to him that I wanted to get a comfortable place to stay during the time I was on the Rhine. He said he knew exactly how I felt and that he thought he could get a very nice and at the same time interesting place for me. On the following day he took me to look at a little house directly on the Rhine which belonged to the von Oswald family.

This family are the great steel and iron people in that part of the country and are very wealthy. The little house

in question was owned by them and was said to have
been built by Napoleon for Josephine when she came up
to the Rhine. It exactly suited me and was a delightful
place. I immediately took steps to have this house requi-
sitioned for my occupancy.

On December 15 we had a beautiful sunshiny day. I took
the opportunity of flying around the country. The banks
of the Moselle are covered with vineyards. Many of the
hills are surmounted by castles, most of them in a ruined
and dilapidated state. It was in this area that the robber
knights and barons maintained their sway in the Middle
Ages. The old castle at Cochem has been entirely restored
by some rich German, who in addition, has built an automobile road up the precipitous sides of the cliff.

General Pershing has established advanced American
headquarters of the A.E.F. at Treves. This has been done
in case anything happens in Germany which requires the
presence of the commanding general, and also as a means
of having a representative of General Headquarters in that
area to look after the line of communications of the Third
American Army on the Rhine.

A number of us general officers were ordered to take our
annual physical examination there on December 17. A pe-
culiar thing that struck me about this was the tremendously
high blood pressure that everybody had. Although I am in
splendid physical condition, my blood pressure is above
normal. General Preston Brown had the highest, although
I do not remember what it was. General Pershing's blood
pressure was up also. This, the doctor told us, is the result
of the severe mental strain which we have been through.
It will gradually go down as our duties and responsibilities
decrease.

My new headquarters at Coblenz is delightful and my
office in one of the municipal buildings is very good. The
windows from this look out over the Rhine toward the castle
of Ehrenbreitstein on the other side. Opposite my desk is a
bust of Julius Cæsar.

It was only a little way below here that Cæsar crossed
the Rhine, and as a result I had to spend many hours of
toil in translating his account of how he placed the bridge

and whipped the Germans. I have selected a place for an airdrome very near the place where he crossed it.

My staff are all busy writing up their views of various phases of aëronautical activities, and I am giving them every opportunity to enjoy themselves and relax from the work which they have been through. We visit the armies adjoining us from time to time. Colonel Rhea, Colonel McCabe, and I ran down to see the British Second Army, which has headquarters at Cologne. Everyone was taking it easy there and pretty much satisfied with things.

The roads are in pretty good shape, but the rolling equipment of the railroads did not look well at all. The French are trying to get all the coal from Germany into France that they can. The coal trains, with the locomotives and railway equipment that are being delivered to the French in accordance with the terms of the Armistice, pass continually.

A day or two afterward we visited the French Tenth Army headquarters at Mainz. There is a good deal of friction everywhere between the German inhabitants and the French. They hate each other, but on the other hand understand each other perfectly, because they have been fighting each other for the last 2,000 years that we know of and probably before that.

We compared our plans of operations with the French, because, of course, if we have trouble with the Germans we shall be under the supreme command of Marshal Foch. When we went to Cologne, the British headquarters, everyone had gone home for Christmas and we found that they had no plans of operation whatever. The French headquarters at Mainz, however, had complete plans in great detail for anything that might come up.

We in the Air Service have worked out our plans of operation just as carefully as it is possible to make them in case of a resumption of hostilities. No matter what happens, the Germans cannot possibly have an air service, as we are taking all of their airplanes. The treaty provided that their new airplanes be delivered to the French, English, and ourselves, and I am accepting several hundred of them at Coblenz. We require certain ones in each lot to be flown by the German pilots. These fliers came down to Coblenz and we have begun the work of accepting the airplanes.

Among the German pilots is Sergeant Donhauser, who is said to be credited with shooting down Lieutenant Quentin Roosevelt during the Château-Thierry operations. He is a little bit of a fellow and has to be lifted into his ship by the mechanics. He is an excellent pilot, however. While trying out one of the airplanes he flattened out too soon, hit a hangar, and had a very bad crash. We sent him to the hospital and I told Paegelow to look after him.

The German airplanes delivered are in very good condition. The Fokkers impress us all very greatly. They can be shipped on the train with their wings off, laid back against the sides of the fuselage. The gas tank remains full of fuel. They can be wheeled off the flat cars, have their wings put on in about fifteen minutes, have the engine cranked up, and they are ready for combat. Even their ammunition belts are full of ammunition. There is no airplane on the Allied side which can be handled in this way. The Fokker fuselage of steel tubing—gas pipes, as our men call them—can be fixed by an ordinary plumber. There is nothing complicated in any way about these splendid airplanes.

Jim Rhea proposed that we take a trip to Wiesbaden the day before Christmas. Pete Bowditch of General Pershing's staff happened to be there with his chief, and we persuaded him to go with us. We had a fine dinner with some friends of Colonel Rhea's and then started back.

It had begun to snow very hard. The windshield of the car was complately covered and it was difficult to find the way along the road. As my chauffeur was very tired, I took the car myself. The road back to Coblenz passes across the Rhine by way of Mainz; that is, it turns to the right after leaving Wiesbaden a few miles. I kept looking for the turn without success, when suddenly we came on a military barracks with a light at the gate and a man with a lance standing guard out in front.

I stopped the car and went over to him. He appeared to be asleep standing up. I asked him in German where the officer of the guard was. This perturbed him very much. He apparently was a recruit. The sergeant of the guard heard the commotion and came out. I told him who we were and where we wanted to go. He told us that we were nearly into Frankfurt am Main, and was very apologetic for the way in which the sentinel had acted.

Of course we were accidentally out of our area and the sergeant could just as well have arrested us if he wanted to. We thanked him very much, turned around, and after driving nearly all night reached Coblenz.

The Christmas season had now arrived. Everybody was preparing for it. We had a little Christmas tree in my quarters and asked many of our friends to come in and partake of cheer of various kinds. Captain Miller of my staff had seen to it that everything that the country produced was provided.

Hazlett, who had been shot down in the Argonne and taken a prisoner, has now rejoined us. He came in as thin as a hungry wolf. He had tried to escape three times, and the last time, when he was climbing under the wire fence, the German sentinel called on him to halt, and when he refused to do so and tried to wiggle through the fence quickly, the sentry stuck him with his bayonet. Hazlett could not sit down for a while after that, and now, if anybody asks him where he was wounded, he hesitates to tell them. I told Hazlett I would appoint him my aide some future day.

I hear that Allan Winslow, who we thought was killed at Château-Thierry, has also come back. I shall appoint him my other aide. Winslow is now minus his left arm, which had to be amputated on account of the wound he received when he was shot down on July 31.

Christmas week of 1918 was a happy one on the Rhine. The troops were all well quartered, well supplied, and were given every privilege commensurate with good discipline. It must be said that the discipline of the American troops cannot be surpassed. Of course there is a great deal of fraternizing with the Germans, as many of our men speak German. There are many orders published that our men should not associate with the citizens, but this does little good.

The English fraternize with the Germans even more than we do. It is funny. A hundred years ago, when Napoleon was the master of Europe and the British and the Germans were fighting together against France, the French were the terrible people committing all sort of atrocities and menacing the peace of the world. Now the Germans are the terrible people and the French and the British are fighting them merely because they are the strongest and upsetting the established order of things.

These same conditions are going to apply in the future as long as the Germans speak German, the French speak French, and the English speak English; and the more we can stay out of their international fights the better it will be for the United States. Our forefathers came from all of these countries to America to escape these very conditions. We must be very careful not to be led back into them on account of the caprices and desire for gain on the part of the financial interests that derive great profit from participation in the affairs of Europe.

We ended up the old year and saw the new year in by having a formal opening of the American Officers' Club in the old German Casino. We had a grand ball and party in which all officers participated, from General Dickman down. This club had been the headquarters for the proprietors of the vineyards and the wine growers of the Moselle and Rhine rivers in this vicinity, and the cellar held the choicest vintages of Germany. These were taken as spoils of war by our victorious army. I think they are the only things we actually captured in Coblenz.

I do not think the wine growers were ever paid for them; at least, they were not up to the time we left, and I was vice president of the club and should know something about it.

Thus ended one of the great years in American history, and with us on the Rhine remained the point of the American spearhead, thrust deeply into the body of Europe. I wonder how soon we shall have to come back to Europe in arms again. I hope never. It is not our place unless we intend to take charge of the destinies of the world, which at this time seems a little premature. I think it is perfectly suitable for us to take over the white man's fight in Asia whenever necessity arises; but to precipitate ourselves into European politics will unquestionably lead to serious political dissensions, if not the breaking up of our principles of government and even of our republic.